Over 100 Tasty Marijuana Treats

Baked 2

By Yzabetta Sativa

GREEN CANDY PRESS

BAKED 2

Published by Green Candy Press

Copyright © 2017 Yzabetta Sativa

ISBN 978-1-937866-38-9

Photographs © Brody Bruce
Additional photography by Herb Kutter

This book contains information about illegal substances, specifically the plant Cannabis and its derivative products. Green Candy Press would like to emphasize that Cannabis is a controlled substance in North America and throughout much of the world. As such, the use and cultivation of cannabis can carry heavy penalties that may threaten an individual's liberty and livelihood.

The aim of the Publisher is to educate and entertain. Whatever the Publisher's view on the validity of current legislation, we do not in any way condone the use of prohibited substances.

Printed in China by Oceanic Graphic International Inc.

Sometimes Massively Distributed by P.G.W.

Contents

Introduction

I clearly remember the cold evening in March when I finally bundled up my insecurities and sent my submission to Green Candy Press. I remember thinking, *Okay, I can't be the only person who doesn't want to have to smoke to get high. This is a good idea; it's worth a try*. Though I never thought the book would get published I resolved to take the gamble, but I also was determined not to let potential rejection get in the way of being as creative as possible when coming up with new and more delicious ways of getting baked.

I claimed in my submission letter I was nothing more than an average individual, who has led a rather non-average life. I mentioned my training in French cuisine as well as admitting that despite a variety of career choices that took me out of the kitchen, I always managed to maintain my passion for cooking. This is more true now that it was that March in 2010 when I sent in my submission for *Baked*.

What truly pushed me to write that cookbook was that I couldn't quit smoking cigarettes without stopping smoking pot as well. When I started experimenting with different recipes, to get high without the lung damage, I asked a lot of people to test my recipes with me, and I discovered that I wasn't the only one with a passion for edibles. Many people would prefer to eat pot rather than smoke it. That was, and still is, my main inspiration for experimenting with more and more delectable recipes.

However, it's not as if I just woke up one morning and started lacing my meals with weed. Far from it. In the 70s, my oldest brother smuggled into the house a cookbook called *The Art and Science of Cooking With Cannabis* by Adam Gottleib. My brothers and I, all potheads, studied this book from cover to cover and I still own this coveted book, published in 1973.

My brothers and I liked nothing more than to crowd in the kitchen to make a marijuana-laced meal. Some of us would do the meal prep and cooking while the rest of us would be on guard, to keep our parents off our scent (if you'll pardon the pun). Often the parents were out coaching hockey teams that none of my brothers played on, so it was relatively easy to get away with these meals.

We'd laugh a lot as a bunch of loving siblings are prone to doing after getting high. We'd cook, we'd eat, and then we'd all hang out in the basement while one played a beat-up old acoustic guitar and a few others would screech out Rush tunes. These half-assed jam sessions make up some of my fondest memories of my wasted adolescence.

The memory of those hazy nights and delicious meals inspired me to take a chance and send in my manuscript—and, to my joy, my recipes piqued the interest of Green Candy Press.

So many wonderful things have happened since the first edition of *Baked* was published. I am still nothing more than an average individual, who has led a rather non-average life, but I love to come up with new recipes and new ways to infuse weed all the time. Pot is such a warm and aromatic yet slightly bitter tasting herb in the hops family, which makes it a challenge to come up with recipes that work well and are enhanced by the pot flavor. However, I am still very intrigued by how many different dishes you can come up with just by following the hops flavor profile. This second edition of *Baked* offers the reader a wide selection of easy and tasty recipes, both sweet and savory; crowd pleasers all around. More than that, it also offers the reader the option of a healthier lifestyle. I started cooking with weed so I could quit smoking and I am more than proud to say that I haven't smoked ANYTHING in almost a decade. You too can make a positive change!

A Wee Bit About Weed

I do most, if not all of my baking, with what is affectionately called BC Bud. The thing is, it is actually grown locally and hydroponically and doesn't come from British Columbia. BC Bud has been parented by a British Columbian clone that sometimes is referred to as White Widow because of how caked in resin the flowers are. This particular strain of weed is a 60% indica / 40% sativa hybrid that is lusciously heady and altogether charming.

Here in Canada there's a lot of smack talk about pot (seeing as it's our second largest agricultural crop), so it's hard to believe anything about the infamous White Widow. My botanically dense, plant-killer mentality thinks that it's really one sub strain or another of Northern Lights—but don't quote me on that.

Indica buds are compact, weighty, short and fat. The thing with indicas is that they smell "skunky" and their smoke is so thick that a small toke can induce coughing. The best indicas have a tranquil sort of "social high" which makes one chill and take in the scenery rather than pseudo-philosophically analyze the scenery to dullard death.

Sativa, on the other hand, has long, medium-thick buds that smell more tangy than sweet; if indica smells "skunky," then sativa smells like dirt or mud. The smoke is smooth and gives a kind of frenetic and confusing high. In short, sativa gets you high and indica gets you stoned. That's pretty much the extent of my scientific knowledge of weed botany.

The most anyone really knows goes as follows: Most of the THC, the medicinal ingredient, is in the flower buds of the female cannabis plant, with some in the leaves too. When I make Baked Butter I use the flower buds of really good pot. One could use the leaves or the stalk as well as what is known as "shake," but you wouldn't get as potent a butter as you wish for. It's a personal choice.

The Disclaimer

Marijuana is illegal whether you smoke it or cook with it

if you don't have a prescription for it

Unless you are lucky enough to live in a state where consumption for recreational purposes has been legalized, marijuana is illegal whether you smoke it or cook with it if you don't have a prescription for it.

Do not eat cannabis and drive. Do not drink and drive. Hell, don't bother driving at all if you can help it, because it puts unnecessary wrinkles on your face.

Know your tolerance, whether you have never tried pot or have been using copious amounts for years. The first time you try eating cannabis-laced food you should eat just a small amount and wait for an hour and a half. At that point you will start feeling the effects of the THC; take note of how you feel and the next time you ingest, adjust the dosage. Always eat the amount recommended in each of the recipes, not more. Eating marijuana gives the same effects as smoking it, but often lasts two or three times longer, which you should keep in mind at all times.

Don't eat pot on an empty stomach. Sure, some people will tell you it's better on an empty stomach but in my opinion it's best to have something to eat beforehand. Even a glass of milk is a good start. Having something in your stomach seems to help prevent you from eating too much or getting hit too hard. To quote Martha Stewart, "It's a good thing."

You must be patient; don't just keep eating your medicated pasta until you feel the effects. I can't say this enough: It will take a while for it to hit you. Make very sure that when you get the munchies you don't eat more. Please do not create a six- or eight-course feast and have every dish include some form of pot. The dishes in this book are designed for consumption with other dishes that don't contain cannabis. If you're making an eight-course extravaganza based on the courses outlined in this book, just have one cannabis-laden dish. Care must be exercised, as the delayed response time when eating pot can encourage overdosing in people who are not used to ingesting marijuana. If you eat too much pot you can feel very rough; experiencing panic and anxiety reactions is bad enough, but

you can also have to endure physical discomfort too.

Absorption of THC though the stomach is slower than through the lungs, which is why you need to be patient. THC gets absorbed at a different rate every time you eat it. It can take well over an hour and a half to be absorbed into the body and for you to feel "high." The effects of eating cannabis can last several hours, while they tend to wear off within an hour when smoked. If you fall asleep or pass out please remember that your digestion will slow down, which means you could wake up still high.

Make no mistake: You can eat far too much pot and the results of that are unpleasant, to say the least. If you do have a dose that is really too high, it can last a long time, possibly as long as ten hours. This is not as fun as it sounds; if you're in the wrong place or with the wrong people it can become very upsetting and you can even pass out. Pot is meant to be fun and relaxing, and dizziness, sweating, nausea, vomiting, possible crying. and freaking out are definitely not fun.

If you do eat too much there are a couple of things you can do. Stay low to the ground, to avoid nasty head rushes, and try taking a high dose of vitamin C (200mg or more) to help to make you feel better. You can also try eating something relatively heavy—a slice of pizza rather than a salad—or something quite sugary. The best antidote is to crawl into bed and go to sleep.

You, as the consumer, have responsibility in three areas: Your situation, your health, and your safety. The situational responsibilities include the avoidance of risky situations, not using it when you're alone and not using it because someone persuasive talked you into it. Health responsibilities include not eating too much or mixing it with other drugs, attentiveness to all the possible health consequences of drug use, and not using a drug recreationally during periods of excessive stress in order to self medicate. If you are self-medicating, in my opinion you have a problem that eating pot isn't going to help. Safety-related responsibilities include using the smallest dose necessary to achieve the desired effects, using only in laid back surroundings with supportive friends, and not doing anything ridiculous like operating heavy machinery after eating pot.

I am highlighting responsible drug use as a chief prevention technique in my personal harm-reduction drug policy and because I care. We all want to enjoy pot, so just don't be stupid and have fun!

Extractions

Baked Butter

It doesn't get better
than this

Place the powdered pot and butter or margarine in a regular crock pot. A mini crock pot (1½-quart) is the best. Regular size crock pots are only good if you're cooking 3 or 4 pounds of Baked Butter or margarine at a time.

Heat the butter or margarine and powdered pot together in the crock pot on low for at least 12 hours but ultimately for 24 hours, covered. Allow the butter or margarine to cool then strain through a strainer, lined with a layer of cheesecloth, into a large bowl. Twist the pulp left in the double layer of cheesecloth to get out all the liquid butter or margarine. Refrigerate to quicken cooling. When cool, cut into large pieces, then place Baked Butter or margarine in sandwich bags for freezing in ½-cup quantities.

I personally don't strain the butter or margarine when it's done, if not out of abject laziness then for the added fiber in my diet. The only thing you have to be careful of, if you choose not to strain, is that ½ cup of butter or margarine with the powdered pot in it does not actually measure ½ cup of butter or margarine. I measure ½ cup plus a dollop, if you will, to even out the score.

It used to be that people would use "shake" or low-grade pot for making Baked Butter. However, more recent studies show that the superiority, potency, and staying power of the final product are greatly improved by

INGREDIENTS

1 pound of butter or margarine (margarine just doesn't work the same but if you're vegan or lactose intolerant then by all means, use vegan margarine)

½ ounce of good pot ground to a powder (grind the pot up by using a coffee grinder, pepper grinder, or blender, though when I do it in a blender I add the butter or margarine, melted, to the blender)

To begin, you will need the pot and the butter.

Grind the pot to a fine powder using a coffee grinder.

Place ingredients into a small crock pot on low heat.

Allow ingredients to melt together, then simmer for over 24 hours.

Over a bowl, pour the ingredients into a strainer.

Squeeze the liquid through, and let the Baked Butter cool.

using good pot as opposed to "shake." In Canada we're able to purchase some wonderful hydroponically grown pot, which is my personal preference.

This Baked Butter or margarine will keep a long time in the freezer and you can use it just as you would use any butter or margarine in any recipe, be it savory or sweet. You can enjoy it in smaller amounts spread on your toast, on your pancakes, or drizzled over popcorn. Each person only needs about 2 teaspoons of Baked Butter or margarine to get totally baked.

"Oregano" Oil
An infusion with a real kick!

Place the powdered pot and oil in a regular crock pot. A mini crock pot (1¹⁄₂-quart) is the best. Regular size crock pots are only good if you're making a lot of "Oregano" Oil at a time. Make sure the heat on the crock pot is set at the lowest it can go.

Heat the oil and powdered pot together in the crock pot on low for at least 12 hours but ultimately for 24 hours, covered. Allow the oil to cool then strain through a strainer, lined with a layer of cheesecloth, into a large bowl. Twist the pulp in the double layer of cheesecloth to get out all the oil. Refrigerate to quicken cooling. When cool, pour the oil back into its bottle, or another clean bottle, making sure to label it; you don't want someone to mistake it for normal oil and accidentally dose themselves.

I personally don't strain the oil when it's done, if not out of abject laziness then for the added fiber in my diet. The only thing you have to be careful of, if you choose not to strain, is that ¹⁄₃ cup of "Oregano" Oil with the powdered pot in it does not actually measure ¹⁄₃ cup of "Oregano" Oil. I measure ¹⁄₃ cup plus a bit more, if you will, to even out the score.

It used to be that people would use "shake" or low-grade pot for making "Oregano" Oil. However, more recent studies show that the superiority, potency and staying power of the final product are greatly improved by

INGREDIENTS

2 cups of olive oil

¹⁄₂ ounce of good pot ground to a powder (grind the pot up by using a coffee grinder)

using good pot as opposed to "shake." In Canada we're able to purchase some wonderful hydroponically grown pot, which is my personal preference.

This "Oregano" Oil will keep a long time in the fridge and you can use it just as you would use any oil in any recipe, be it savory or sweet. You can enjoy it in the same regard that you would any other oil. Olive oil is the main cooking oil in countries surrounding the Mediterranean Sea.

Extra virgin olive oil is mostly used as a salad dressing and as an ingredient in salad dressings. It is also used with foods to be eaten cold. If uncompromised by heat, the flavor is stronger. It also can be used for sautéing.

Cannabis Coconut Oil

A healthier way to get high.

Place powdered pot and oil in a regular crock pot. A mini crock pot (1½-quart) is the best. Regular size crock pots are only good if you're cooking lots of oil at a time. Make sure the heat on the crock pot is the lowest it can go.

Heat the oil and powdered pot together in the crock pot on low at least 12 hours but ultimately for 24 hours, covered. Strain the cooled oil through a strainer, lined with a layer of cheesecloth, into the large bowl. Twist the pulp in the double layer of cheesecloth to get out all the oil. Refrigerate to quicken cooling; the oil will solidify as it gets colder. When cool, cut into large pieces, and place the pieces in sandwich bags for freezing in ⅓-cup quantities.

I personally don't strain the oil when it's done, if not out of abject laziness then for the added fiber in my diet. The only thing you have to be careful of, if you choose not to strain, is that a ⅓ cup of oil with the powdered pot in it does not actually measure ⅓ cup of oil. I measure ⅓ cup plus a little more, if you will, to even out the score.

It used to be that people would use "shake" or low-grade pot for making Cannabis Coconut Oil. However, more recent studies show that the superiority, potency and staying power of the pot are greatly improved

INGREDIENTS

2 cups of coconut oil

½ an ounce of good pot ground to a powder (grind the pot up by using a coffee grinder)

with good pot as opposed to "shake." In Canada we're able to purchase some wonderful hydroponically grown, pot, which has been my personal preference.

This coconut oil will keep a long time in the freezer and you can use it just as you would use any oil in any recipe, be it savory or sweet. You can enjoy it in the same regard as you would any other oil, and even use it in the place of butter in some sweet recipes.

Baked Lard (or Shortening)

Your grandma's favorite way to get baked

Place powdered pot and lard or shortening in a regular crock pot. A mini crock pot (1½-quart) is the best. Regular size crock pots are only good if you're cooking lots of lard or shortening at a time.

Heat the lard or shortening and powdered pot together in the crock pot on low at least 12 hours but ultimately for 24 hours, covered. Strain the cooled lard or shortening through a strainer, lined with a layer of cheese-cloth, into a large bowl. Twist the pulp in the double layer of cheesecloth to get out all the liquid lard or shortening you can. Refrigerate to quicken cooling. When cool, cut into large pieces and place the pieces in sandwich bags for freezing in ½-cup quantities.

I personally don't strain the lard or shortening when it's done, if not out of abject laziness then for the added fiber in my diet. The only thing you have to be careful of, if you choose not to strain, is that ½ cup of lard or short-ening with the powdered pot in it does not actually measure ½ cup of lard or shortening. I measure ½ cup plus a dollop, if you will, to even out the score.

Baked Lard or Shortening will keep a long time in the freezer and you can use it just as you would use any lard or shortening in any recipe, be it savory or sweet. Each person only needs about 1 tablespoon of lard or shortening to get baked.

INGREDIENTS

1 pound of lard or shortening
½ ounce of good pot ground to a powder (grind the pot up by using a coffee grinder)

Marijuana Milk (or Cream)

Bringing a whole new meaning to the concept of milk and cookies

Place the powdered pot and milk or cream in a regular crock pot. Set the crock pot on high until the milk or cream is just about to boil, then turn the temperature down to low. Crock pots take an hour or two to get to the boiling stage, so you can always speed up the process by heating up the milk or cream in the microwave or in a pot on the stove before adding it to the crock pot with the weed.

Heat the milk or cream and powdered pot together in the crock pot on low for at least 10 hours, stirring every hour.

When the milk or cream is infused, it will become a medium brownish color, not unlike coffee mocha or the color of a Brown Cow. If the milk or cream is still a beige color, keep it cooking for longer.

Allow the milk or cream to cool then strain through a strainer, lined with a layer of cheesecloth, into a large bowl. Twist the pulp in the double layer of cheesecloth to get out all the liquid. Refrigerate once the milk or cream has cooled. Store in the refrigerator.

You can also make this recipe using coconut milk, for a non-dairy alternative. ⅓ cup of Marijuana Milk or Cream is enough to get you baked.

INGREDIENTS

½ ounce of good pot ground to a powder (grind the pot up by using a coffee grinder)

10 cups of whole milk (alternatively use half-and-half or whipping cream, as it's the fat that brings out the THC)

Alcohol Extractions

A knockout in every single shot

The pot you're using must be dry. When fresh pot is used, the end result has a tendency to be substandard.

If possible, use an empty 1.5-liter wine bottle with a screw-top lid.

Pour the alcohol and ground pot into the empty wine bottle. Keep the empty alcohol bottle for later. Screw the lid tightly onto the bottle and let it sit for two weeks at room temperature in a dark cabinet. Twice a week you need to shake the bottle up so as to agitate the pot.

Using a coffee filter or fine sieve, strain the pot from the alcohol. Put the alcohol back into its original bottle and screw the lid tightly onto the bottle.

It's best to keep the Alcohol Extraction in a cool dark place to protect it from degradation by light. 1 shot is enough to get you baked.

As this extract is alcoholic, you need to be careful with your consumption; because it's alcohol with cannabis in it, you need to be even more careful. For every alcoholic beverage you drink make sure you drink a pint of water—and this goes for alcohol without weed in it, too!

INGREDIENTS

- 750ml bottle of vodka, gin, bourbon, Campari, or white rum (of the highest proof possible in your area)
- ½ ounce of good pot (ground to a powder)

Staples

Burner Bread

For toast that gets you toasted!

Dissolve the yeast in a small bowl with the warm water.

In a large bowl, mix together the Baked Butter, sugar, salt, and hot Marijuana Milk. Stir to dissolve all of the sugar.

Let mixture cool to lukewarm.

Stir in 1½ cups of the flour and mix well. Add the yeast mixture and the beaten eggs and mix together. Add enough of the leftover flour to make a soft but firm dough. Turn out onto a lightly floured surface and knead for about 10 minutes, until the dough is smooth and elastic.

Place the dough in a lightly oiled bowl, turning once to grease the entire surface of the dough. Cover the bowl with a clean dishcloth and let stand in a warm, draft-free place until the dough doubles in mass. This should take about 1½ hours.

Punch the dough down and divide it into two dough balls. Cover both and let them rest for 10 minutes or so.

Preheat oven to 375°F. Grease two 8 x 4 x 3-inch loaf pans.

INGREDIENTS

1 package of active dry yeast

¼ cup of lukewarm water

¼ cup of Baked Butter (page 13)

¼ cup of brown sugar

1½ teaspoons of salt

½ cup of scalded Marijuana Milk (page 27)

3¾ cups of flour

2 beaten eggs

Shape them into two loaves and place them in the two greased loaf pans. Cover and let the dough rise again for about 45 to 60 minutes, until it has almost doubled.

Bake for 25 minutes, placing foil over the loaves for the last 10 minutes if they are getting too brown. Remove the loaves from the pans and let cool on racks. 2 slices are enough to get you baked.

Cannabis Cider Vinegar

A tablespoon a day keeps the doctor away!

If possible, use an empty 1.5-liter wine bottle with a screw-top lid.

Pour the vinegar and ground pot into the empty wine bottle. Keep the empty vinegar bottle for later. Screw the lid tightly onto the bottle and let it sit two weeks at room temperature in a dark cabinet. Twice a week you need to shake the bottle up so as to agitate the pot.

Using a coffee filter or fine sieve, strain the pot from the vinegar. Put the vinegar back into its original bottle and screw the lid tightly onto the bottle.

This vinegar will keep a long time in the fridge and you can use it just as you would use any cider vinegar in any recipe.

3 tablespoons of this vinegar are enough to get you baked.

INGREDIENTS

6 cups of apple cider vinegar
(though any kind of vinegar works)
$1/2$ ounce of good pot ground to a
powder (grind the pot up by using
a coffee grinder)

Baked Buttermilk

Curdle your consciousness!

Combine the milk and lemon juice or white vinegar.

Let the mixture stand at room temperature for 5 to 10 minutes. When it is ready, the milk will be slightly thickened and you will see small, curdled bits. This buttermilk will not become as thick as regular buttermilk.

Use this substitute (including curdled bits) as you would buttermilk in your recipe.

1/3 cup of this buttermilk is enough to get you baked.

1 cup of Marijuana Milk (page 27)

1 tablespoon of lemon juice or white vinegar

Chronic Cheese

Dairy that Dre
would be proud of

Pour the Marijuana Milk into a stainless steel saucepan and cook over a medium heat until it reaches 200°F.

Slowly stir in the lemon juice. Remove the pot from heat and allow the mixture to curdle (sounds gross, I know). Let cool until it's not too hot to touch.

Pour the cheese into cloth-lined bowl. Cheesecloth would be perfect for this but a clean pillowcase will do in a pinch. Pull together the 4 corners of cloth or the top of the pillowcase and twist it around a spoon.

Hang the dripping cheese for a few hours at least.

Season to taste and check consistency. I like a fairly hard cheese, so I hang it in the fridge overnight.

When the cheese has reached the desired consistency, untie the pillow-case or cheesecloth and remove the cheese from the cloth. Place the cheese in an airtight container, and let it chill.

1/3 cup of this cheese is enough to get you baked.

INGREDIENTS

8 cups of Marijuana Milk (page 27)
1/4 cup of fresh lemon juice
salt to taste

Baked Yogurt
Because your good bacteria
deserves to get high too

Pour the Marijuana Milk into a large, heavy cooking pot with a lid and set over medium to medium-high heat. Warm the milk to just below boiling, which is about 200°F. Stir the milk gently and often as you heat it up, to make sure the bottom doesn't burn and the milk doesn't boil over.

Let the milk cool until it is just warm to the touch, around 112°F to 115°F. Stir occasionally to prevent a skin from forming. You can help speed this up by placing the pot in an ice water bath and gently stirring the milk until it cools to the right temperature.

Scoop out about a cup of warm milk from the cooking pot, pour it into a bowl and add the yogurt. Whisk together until it's smooth and the yogurt is well incorporated into the milk.

Whisk the thinned yogurt back into the milk in the pot. Make sure you whisk continuously and gently while pouring the yogurt mixture into the warmed milk in a steady stream.

Cover the pot with the lid and place the whole pot in a turned-off oven. Wrap the pot in towels to keep the milk warm as it sets. It should ideally be around 110°F, though some inconsistency is fine.

INGREDIENTS

8 cups of Marijuana Milk (page 27)

½ cup of plain yogurt containing active cultures (Activia by Dannon, for example)

Let the yogurt set for at least 4 hours or as long as overnight. The exact time will depend on the cultures used, the temperature of the yogurt, and your yogurt preferences. The longer the yogurt sits, the thicker and more tart it becomes. If this is your first time making yogurt, start checking it after 4 hours and stop when it reaches a flavor and consistency you like. Avoid manhandling or stirring the yogurt until it has fully set.

Once the yogurt has set to your liking, remove it from the oven. If you see any watery whey on the surface of the yogurt, you can either drain this off or whisk it back into the yogurt before placing the yogurt into storage containers. Whisking also gives the yogurt a more consistent creamy texture.

Transfer the yogurt to storage containers, cover and refrigerate. Home-made yogurt will keep for about 2 weeks in the refrigerator.

$1/2$ cup of this yogurt is enough to get you baked.

Cannabis Chili Oil

A spicy twist on infused oil

Place the powdered pot, chili peppers, crushed red pepper, and oil in a mini crock pot on the lowest heat setting. A mini crock pot (1½-quart) is the best. Regular size crock pots are only good if you're cooking a lot of oil at once.

Heat the oil and powdered pot together in the crock pot on low for at least 12 hours but ultimately for 24 hours, covered. Line a strainer with a layer of cheesecloth and strain the cooled oil into a large bowl. Twist the pulp in the double layer of cheesecloth to get out all the oil. Refrigerate to quicken cooling.

When cool, pour the oil back into its bottle, or another clean bottle, making sure to label it; you don't want someone to mistake it for normal oil and accidentally dose themselves.

This oil will keep a long time in the fridge and you can use it as you would any other chili oil.

1 tablespoon of Cannabis Chili Oil is enough to get you baked.

INGREDIENTS

2 cups of olive oil

½ ounce of good pot ground to a powder (grind the pot up by using a coffee grinder)

7 dried Chiles de Arbol

1½ teaspoons of crushed red pepper

Fried Fish Sauce

For Thai food that gets you high!

If possible, use an empty 1.5-liter wine bottle with a screw-top lid.

Pour the fish sauce and ground pot into the empty wine bottle. Keep the empty fish sauce bottle for later. Screw the lid tightly onto the bottle and let it sit for 4 weeks at room temperature in a dark cabinet. Twice a week, shake the bottle up so as to agitate the pot.

After 4 weeks, strain the pot from the fish sauce using a coffee filter or fine sieve. Put the fish sauce back into its original bottle and screw the lid tightly onto the bottle.

It's best to keep the Fried Fish Sauce in the fridge. 2 tablespoons of Fried Fish Sauce are enough to get you baked.

1 750ml bottle of fish sauce

1/2 ounce of good pot ground to a powder (grind the pot up by using a coffee grinder)

Cannabis Coleslaw Dressing

Get pickled!

In a saucepan over medium heat, combine all of the ingredients, stir well, and bring the mixture to a boil. Lower the heat and simmer, stirring until all of the sugar dissolves. Remove from the heat and let cool.

2 tablespoons of Cannabis Coleslaw Dressing are enough to get you baked.

INGREDIENTS

3/4 cup of brown sugar

1 teaspoon of salt

2/3 cup of "Oregano" Oil (page 17)

1 teaspoon of dry mustard

1 teaspoon of celery seed

1 cup of Cannabis Cider Vinegar
   (page 37)

Mary Jane Mayo
The real thing, now medicated!

Mix the egg, garlic, lime juice, and Dijon mustard together in a blender or food processor. Blend until smooth, then blend on low speed while pouring the "Oregano" Oil into the blender in a fine stream as the mixture emulsifies and thickens.

Keep refrigerated.

1 tablespoon of MJ Mayo is enough to get you baked.

INGREDIENTS

1 egg

1/2 teaspoon of finely minced garlic

1 tablespoon of freshly squeezed
   lime juice

1 teaspoon of prepared Dijon
   mustard

3/4 cup of "Oregano" Oil (page 17)

sea salt and fresh cracked black
   pepper to taste

Marijuana Mustard

Tangy, tasty and
good with everything!

Soak the mustard seeds in the vinegar and water, making sure the liquid entirely covers the seeds. Leave these seeds soaking for 2 full days.

Blend the seed mixture along with the sugar in a food processor until it reaches the desired consistency, adding water if needed. The mustard will seem hot at first, but will mellow out after a day or two in the fridge.

3 tablespoons of Marijuana Mustard are enough to get one person baked. Be careful not to ingest too many infused condiments at one meal.

INGREDIENTS

1 teaspoon of brown sugar

1 cup of Cannabis Cider Vinegar
   (page 37)

1/2 cup of mustard seeds

1/3 cup of water

Cannaketchup
It's not the bottled stuff. It's better

Place all the raw vegetables in a large, heavy-bottomed saucepan with a big splash of "Oregano" Oil, stir, then add the spices. Season well with salt and pepper. Cook this mixture moderately over a low heat for 10 to 15 minutes until softened, stirring every so often.

Add the puréed tomatoes, the rest of the "Oregano" Oil, and the cold water. Bring all of this to a boil, reduce the heat, and simmer gently until the sauce reduces by half.

Remove the tomato mixture from the heat and, with an immersion blender or in a food processor, blend everything together until smooth. Push the tomato mixture through a fine sieve at least twice, to make it smooth and shiny.

Put the sauce into a clean pan and add the Cannabis Cider Vinegar along with the sugar and tomato paste. Place the sauce over medium heat and simmer until it reduces and thickens to the consistency of tomato ketchup. At this point, correct the seasoning to taste.

Store the ketchup in the refrigerator. 2 tablespoons of Cannaketchup are enough to get 1 person baked. Be careful not to ingest too many infused condiments at one meal.

INGREDIENTS

1 (28oz) can of puréed tomatoes

1 large red onion, chopped

1/3 cup of "Oregano" Oil (page 17)

1 tablespoon of tomato paste
   (maybe two)

2/3 cup of packed dark brown sugar

1/2 cup of Cannabis Cider Vinegar
   (page 37)

2 stalks of celery, chopped

3 tablespoons of fresh ginger, peeled
   chopped

2 cloves of garlic, peeled and sliced

1 1/2 cups of cold water

sea salt and pepper to taste

Pot Peanut Butter

PB & J sandwiches
have never been so good

Place the powdered pot, canola oil, and peanut butter in a regular crock pot. A mini crock pot (1½-quart) is the best. Regular size crock pots are only good if you're cooking a lot of peanut butter at a time. Set the crock pot on a low heat.

Heat all the ingredients together for at least 6 to 8 hours, stirring every hour.

When the peanut butter is infused, it will become a medium golden brown color, not unlike the color of a baked peanut butter cookie.

Let cool, then place in a glass jar for storage. Store in the refrigerator. 1 tablespoon of Pot Peanut Butter is enough to get you baked.

INGREDIENTS

- ½ ounce of good pot ground to a powder (grind the pot up by using a coffee grinder)
- 2 ¼ cups of high fat (16 grams or more) peanut butter. Do NOT use crunchy peanut butter or reduced fat peanut butter
- ¼ cup of canola oil

Pot Pesto

Pair with pasta for
a great munchies meal

Combine all the ingredients in blender or food processor with the lid on tightly. Blend the pesto at a medium speed for about 4 minutes, stopping occasionally to scrape the sides of the blender, until the mixture is smooth.

2 tablespoons of Pot Pesto are enough to get you baked.

3 cups of basil leaves (fresh leaves only)

1 cup of grated Parmesan

3/4 cup of "Oregano" Oil (page 17)

2 tablespoons of water

4 ground cloves of garlic

1/4 cup of pistachios

Breakfast

Cannacorn Bread

A classic American breakfast
with a twist

Preheat oven to 400 °F. Grease a 13 x 9 x 2-inch baking pan.

In a mixing bowl, cream together the Baked Butter and sugar. Combine the eggs and milk, add them to the butter mixture, and mix thoroughly.

In another bowl combine the flour, cornmeal, baking powder, and salt. Whisk together for a minute or so with a wire whisk.

Add the dry ingredients to butter mixture and mix well.

Pour the batter into the greased baking pan. Bake for 22-27 minutes or until a toothpick inserted near the center comes out clean. A slightly moist toothpick is ideal, as cornbread can be really dry if you're not careful.

Cut into 16 squares. Serve warm. 1 square of Cannacorn Bread is enough to get you baked.

INGREDIENTS

1/2 cup of Baked Butter (page 13), softened

3/4 cup of sugar

3 eggs

1 2/3 cups of Marijuana Milk made with whole milk or cream (page 27)

2 1/3 cups of all-purpose flour

1 cup of cornmeal

4 1/2 teaspoons of baking powder

1 teaspoon of sea salt

Lammas Bread
From Anglo-Saxon England with love

Preheat oven to 400°F. Flour your breadboard or work space. Grease a cookie sheet.

Place the flour and softened Baked Butter into a large mixing bowl. With a pastry blender or 2 knives, cut the Baked Butter into the flour until the mixture resembles cornmeal. Add the sugar and cut in quickly with the knives so the butter doesn't melt.

In a small bowl, beat the egg, Marijuana Milk and cream together until well combined. Save about a tablespoon of this egg mixture to brush the tops of the Lammas. Add the rest of the egg mixture to the rest of flour and butter and mix just until combined into a soft dough.

Knead the dough 3 or 4 times on a lightly floured surface. Roll dough to a ³/₄-inch thickness and then shape it like a stick figure, as shown. Place on a lightly greased cookie sheet and brush the tops of the Lammas with the reserved egg mixture.

Bake the Lammas for 20-25 minutes in the oven. 1 limb of a Lammas Bread stick figure should be enough to get you baked.

INGREDIENTS

6 tablespoons of Baked Butter
   (page 13), slightly softened
1 egg, well beaten
1 tablespoon of dark brown sugar
¹/₂ cup of Marijuana Milk (page 27)
4 tablespoons of cream
2 cups of self-rising flour

Chronic Peach Compote

Because yogurt deserves better than boring

Bring a pot of water to the boil.

To peel the peaches in close-to-efficient manner, start by cutting a hash-tag in to the bottom of each one. Immerse each peach in boiling water for a moment then pull it out and set it aside. The skin should pare back easily once the peach is cool enough to touch. You can put them in the freezer to cool them quickly but you have to be really careful to make sure they don't get too cold or freeze.

Slice the peaches, trying to catch all the juices from the fruit. Put the peach juice in a saucepan. Add the sugar, orange juice, lime leaf, and cinnamon stick, then simmer until the sauce starts to thicken, which should take about 10 minutes or so. Remove the saucepan from the heat and carefully add the Baked Bourbon into the sauce.

Return the sauce to the heat. Stir in the peaches and cook for 8 minutes.

Remove the pan from the heat and let the peaches sit in the syrup for at least half an hour so that the flavors can develop.

Serve over the Stackhouse Pancakes or with Baked Yogurt and granola. This Chronic Peach Compote is enough to get 2 people baked.

INGREDIENTS

6 fresh freestone peaches

1/3 cup of brown sugar

1/2 cup of freshly squeezed true blood orange juice

1/4 cup of Baked Bourbon, made via the Alcohol Extraction method (page 29)

1 kaffir lime leaf, preferably fresh

1 cinnamon stick

Stackhouse Pancakes

There's no better way
to start the day

Mix all the dry ingredients and the lemon peel together in a large bowl.

Mix the eggs and the Baked Buttermilk together in a smaller bowl.

Melt the Baked Butter, let cool slightly, and then add it slowly to the buttermilk and egg mixture. Whisk this mixture well.

Add the wet ingredients to the dry ingredients and mix; but not very thoroughly, just to moisten all the dry ingredients. The batter can be a bit lumpy; indeed, it should be a wee bit lumpy.

Heat the frying pan until a drop of water fizzes and bounces off.

Brush or swirl the around the bottom of the frying pan with the canola oil, then spoon the batter into the pan, leaving a generous gap between each pancake.

When the top of the pancake starts bubbling, flip it over. Keep an eye on them while you're frying as this only takes about a minute and a half. Cook the other side for another minute.

Keep them warm in the oven until you want to serve.

INGREDIENTS

2 cups of all-purpose flour

2 teaspoons of baking powder

1 teaspoon of baking soda

1/2 teaspoon of salt

3 tablespoons of sugar

1 teaspoon of freshly grated lemon
   peel

2 eggs

4 tablespoons of Baked Butter
   (page 13)

3 cups of Baked Buttermilk (page 39)

canola oil for cooking

Stack about 3 to 4 pancakes on a plate with a dollop of Baked Butter in between each pancake. Top with Chronic Peach Compote (page 69) and maybe some real Canadian maple syrup on the side. 1 stack of Stackhouse Pancakes is enough to get you baked.

Breakfast Fuel

To get you up and out
on those tough mornings

Grease a 9 x 13-inch pan with Baked Butter.

Butter 6 slices of bread and lay them wet side down in the baking pan.

Spread the 4 cups of ham, beef, or tofu over the buttered bread. Lay the slices of cheese on top of this, alternating the mozzarella with the cheddar. Butter the last 6 slices of bread and lay them wet side up in the baking pan on the top of the cheese slices, not unlike lasagna.

In a large measuring cup, whisk the eggs together with the Marijuana Milk, and salt and pepper to taste. Pour the egg mixture over the bread mixture, cover it, and let it chill in the fridge overnight.

In the morning, preheat oven to 350°F.

Remove the cover and sprinkle the Corn Flake crumbs over the top of the mixture.

Gently drizzle the melted Baked Butter over the top of the crumbs as evenly as possible.

Bake for half an hour on the middle rack. Remove from the oven and let

INGREDIENTS

12 slices of muesli bread, or Burner Bread (page 33) if you prefer

2 tablespoons of butter

4 cups of diced ham (or corned beef, or tofu)

6 eggs

1/2 cup of Marijuana Milk (page 27)

1 cup of Corn Flakes, smashed to crumbs

3 slices of real mozzarella

3 slices of real cheddar

1/2 cup of Baked Butter (page 13), melted

sit for about 5 minutes to make it easier to slice. Cut the fuel into 10 even pieces.

1 piece of Breakfast Fuel is enough to start your morning off right and get you baked.

If you've used Burner Bread instead of muesli bread, be aware that this recipe will contain more marijuana and therefore be stronger.

Mary Jane Farls

A Scottish bread roll
with a cannabis twist

Preheat a flat griddle pan or skillet on medium to low heat.

Place the flour and salt in a bowl and sift in the baking soda. Make a well in the center, and pour in the Baked Buttermilk.

Work quickly to mix into a dough and knead very lightly on a well-floured surface. Form into a flattened circle, about ¹/₂-inch thick, and cut into quarters with a floured knife.

Sprinkle a little flour over the base of the hot pan and cook the farls for 6 to 8 minutes on each side or until golden brown.

1 Mary Jane Farl (one quarter of the whole dough) is enough to get you baked, especially if you spread it with Pot Peanut Butter (page 59) or Baked Butter (page 13).

INGREDIENTS

2 cups of all-purpose flour

¹/₂ teaspoon of salt

1 teaspoon of baking soda

1 cup of Baked Buttermilk (page 39)

Irish Soda Bread

A slice of the Emerald Isle!

Preheat oven to 350°F.

In a large bowl mix the flour, brown sugar, baking powder, baking soda, and salt. Cut in the Baked Butter with a pastry blender or two knives until the mixture resembles coarse crumbs.

Add the Baked Buttermilk, orange juice and orange peel. Stir just until combined.

On a lightly floured surface, knead the dough 15 times. Shape into 2 round loaves, about an inch thick. Place them on a baking sheet sprayed with cooking spray.

Cut a deep *X* in the top of the dough just like you would with hot cross buns. Sprinkle the *X* with brown sugar.

Bake the bread for 50 minutes or until golden brown. Remove from the baking sheet onto a wire rack. Allow to cool completely before cutting into wedges. Cut each loaf into 6 wedges.

1 wedge of Irish Soda Bread is enough to get you baked.

INGREDIENTS

3 1/4 cups of flour

1/3 cup of brown sugar

1 teaspoon of baking powder

1 teaspoon of baking soda

1 teaspoon of salt

1/2 cup of cold Baked Butter
   (page 13), cut up

1 cup of Baked Buttermilk (page 39)

1/3 cup of orange juice

1/2 teaspoon of grated orange peel

brown sugar for garnish

Baked French Toast

A decadent breakfast
from the continent

Preheat oven to 325°F.

On baking sheet, toast the cashews in the oven for about 5 minutes. Set aside.

Turn the oven up to 350°F.

In large bowl, whisk together the eggs, Marijuana Milk, maple syrup, cinnamon, vanilla, and salt. Cut the bread into 3/4-inch thick slices. Dip the bread into the egg mixture until soaked.

In a large frying pan, melt 1 tablespoon of the Baked Butter over medium heat. Fry the bread, in batches, adding more Baked Butter as needed, until golden. It takes about 3 minutes for each slice to fry.

Transfer the toast to 2 baking sheets. Bake the slices in oven until puffed and heated through. This takes about 5 minutes.

FOR THE CARAMELIZED BANANAS

While the toast is baking, melt half of the Baked Butter in a large frying pan over medium-high heat. Fry half of the bananas, turning once, until golden in color and tender. Transfer to plate. Repeat this process with the rest of the bananas.

INGREDIENTS

1/3 cup of roughly chopped cashews

6 eggs

1 1/2 cups of Marijuana Milk (page 27)

2 tablespoons of maple syrup

1 teaspoon of ground cinnamon

1 teaspoon of pure vanilla extract

a pinch of salt

1 loaf of Burner Bread (page 33) or
    Irish Soda Bread (page 81)

2 tablespoons of Baked Butter
    (page 13)

FOR THE CARAMELIZED BANANAS

2 tablespoons of Baked Butter
    (page 13)

6 firm ripe bananas, sliced in half,
    with each half cut into two

1/2 cup of maple syrup

1/2 cup of golden corn syrup

1/3 cup of Baked Bourbon or Wasted
    White Rum, made via the Alcohol
    Extraction method (page 29).

In the same frying pan, bring the maple syrup, sugar, corn syrup, and Baked Bourbon to a slow boil over medium-high heat. Reduce the heat and simmer the sauce for 2 minutes. Gently stir in the bananas. Simmer them in the sauce for 1 minute.

When the bread is baked, spoon the caramelized bananas over the Baked French Toast. Sprinkle with the toasted cashews and serve immediately.

This recipe is enough to get 6 people baked.

Baked Breakfast Nog

A nog is for life, not just for Christmas!

Mix all ingredients in a blender then transfer the mixture to a large pot over a low heat.

Heat slowly, whisking constantly, until the mixture is just about to boil (about 6 minutes). Remove the nog from the heat. You'll know it's ready when it starts to thicken to the consistency of store-bought eggnog.

Let cool, then refrigerate overnight.

To serve, add a splash of heavy cream and garnish with a sprinkle of cinnamon.

One glass of Baked Breakfast Nog is enough to get you baked, especially if you add some Wasted White Rum or Baked Bourbon made via the Alcohol Extraction method (page 29).

INGREDIENTS

4 cups of Marijuana Milk (page 27)

1 teaspoon of pure vanilla extract

1/2 teaspoon of ground cinnamon

6 tablespoons of whole egg powder
   or 6 whole eggs

1/2 cup of granulated sugar

Lunch

Spicy Stoner Slaw

A healthy side dish—made better!

Place all the dressing ingredients into a blender and blend until smooth.

Combine all the slaw ingredients in a large bowl, toss with the dressing, and season with salt and pepper. Serve immediately.

This recipe is enough to get 8 people baked.

INGREDIENTS

FOR THE DRESSING

1/2 cup of "Oregano" Oil (page 17)

1/3 cup of fresh lime juice

1/3 teaspoon of ground cumin

1/3 teaspoon of ground paprika

1/3 teaspoon of crushed chili
    peppers

1 clove of garlic, minced finely

FOR THE SLAW

2 carrots, peeled and shredded

1 medium head of green cabbage,
    shredded

1 1/2 cups of shredded Brussels sprouts

1 red onion, thinly sliced

1/2 cup of chopped, fresh cilantro

salt and pepper

Ganja Gazpacho

A cold nut soup from Malaga—now with pot!

Place the almonds, grapes, apple, pine nuts, garlic, Marijuana Milk, white wine vinegar and half the croutons in a blender.

Pulse about 10 times, and then blend the soup at high speed for 90 seconds. If necessary, add more croutons to adjust the consistency. The mixture should be about as thick as pea soup.

Pass the soup through a strainer, pressing the bits through with the back of a wooden spoon. Discard the goop and refrigerate the soup for at least 2 hours.

Just before serving, add the cream and season to taste.

Serve the gazpacho in chilled soup bowls, garnished with sliced almonds, julienned cucumber, and a drizzle of olive oil.

This recipe is enough to get 4 people baked.

INGREDIENTS

1/2 cup of blanched whole almonds

1 1/4 cups of seedless green grapes, halved

1 Granny Smith apple, peeled, cored, and diced

2 tablespoons of pine nuts

1 clove of garlic, finely chopped

3/4 cup of Marijuana Milk (page 27)

2 tablespoons of white wine vinegar

1 1/2 cups of croutons

1/3 cup of whipping cream

TO GARNISH

3 tablespoons of toasted sliced almonds

3 tablespoons of English cucumber, julienned

olive oil

Baked Eggplant Casserole

Creamy, delicious, and guaranteed
to get you high.

Preheat oven to 350°F.

Lay the sliced eggplant out on a paper towel. Sprinkle the eggplant with salt and let stand for 30 minutes. After 30 minutes, wipe the eggplant off with a paper towel but do not run it under water.

Heat the "Oregano" Oil in a large frying pan and fry the eggplant slices to a light brown color. Remove from the pan and allow to cool.

In a medium bowl, mix the Chronic Cheese, mozzarella, and 1/4 cup of the Parmesan. Mix in the egg and basil.

In a 13 x 9-inch glass baking dish, evenly spread half the marinara sauce. Arrange a single layer of eggplant slices on top of the sauce. Top the eggplant with 1/2 cup of the cheese mixture. Repeat this layering process until all the eggplant and cheese mixture is used.

Pour the remaining sauce on top of the layers, and sprinkle with the remaining Parmesan.

Bake the eggplant for 30 to 45 minutes until the sauce is bubbly. Let stand for 5 minutes then serve. This recipe is enough to get 4 people baked.

INGREDIENTS

1/3 cup of "Oregano" Oil (page 17)

6 eggplants, cut into 1/4-inch slices

1 cup of Chronic Cheese (page 41)

1 cup of shredded mozzarella

1/4 cup of grated Parmesan

1 egg, beaten

1/3 cup of chopped fresh basil

6 cups of marinara sauce

sea salt

Mac 'n' Cheese Muffins

Comfort food that's now infused

Preheat oven to 375°F.

Butter a muffin pan and divide the breadcrumbs between the cups. Shake and tilt the pan to coat all sides of the cups well. Discard whatever is left loose in the muffin pan. Bring a large pot of salted water to the boil. Add in the macaroni and cook for about 8 minutes, or until al dente. Let the macaroni cool and set aside.

In a saucepan over medium heat, melt the Baked Butter. Add in the flour, mustard, salt, and pepper. Cook this roux for about a minute, whisking gently. Gradually whisk in the Marijuana Milk.

Once the milk is fully incorporated and there are no lumps, bring the mixture to a boil and then reduce the heat. Whisk for 3 to 5 minutes or until the mixture is smooth and thickened. Remove the saucepan from the heat, stir in 2 cups of the Old Cheddar and stir until smooth.

Return the macaroni to the pot. Pour the cheese sauce over the pasta, and stir until well coated. Divide the mixture evenly among the muffin cups. Sprinkle with the remaining cheese. Bake for 20 minutes or until hot. Let the muffins stand for 10 minutes. Run a small knife around each muffin, then ease each one out of the cup. One Mac 'n' Cheese Muffin is enough to get you baked.

INGREDIENTS

2 tablespoons of dry breadcrumbs

2 1/2 cups of elbow macaroni

3 tablespoons of Baked Butter (page 13)

3 tablespoons of all-purpose flour

1 1/2 teaspoons of dry mustard

1/2 teaspoon of salt

1/4 teaspoon of pepper

1 1/2 cups of Marijuana Milk (page 27)

2 1/2 cups of grated Old Cheddar

Cornucopian Vegetable Salad

Your five a day in a brand new way

In a large salad bowl, combine the broccoli, cauliflower, tomatoes, cucumber, onion, carrots, and both types of olives.

In a small bowl, whisk together the Mary Jane Mayo, vinegar, lemon juice, oil, Worcestershire sauce, oregano, basil, sugar, and garlic until evenly combined.

Pour the salad dressing over the vegetable mixture and toss to coat. Cover and refrigerate for at least 4 hours. Stir in the mozzarella just before serving.

This recipe is enough to get 6 people baked.

INGREDIENTS

1 head of broccoli, broken into florets

1 head of cauliflower, broken into florets

2 cups of cherry tomatoes

1 medium English cucumber, sliced

1 medium Vidalia onion, thinly sliced

1 cup of fresh carrots, sliced

1 cup of ripe olives, drained and sliced

1/2 cup of pimiento-stuffed olives

1/2 cup of Mary Jane Mayo (page 53)

2 tablespoons of red wine vinegar

3 tablespoons of fresh lemon juice

1/3 cup of "Oregano" Oil (page 17)

1 teaspoon of Worcestershire sauce

1 teaspoon of dried oregano

1 teaspoon of dried basil

1 1/2 teaspoons of white sugar

2 ground cloves of garlic, chopped

2 cups of mozzarella, shredded

Baked Brain Beans

A Boston classic, now with bud!

Drain the soaked beans. Place into a large pot with fresh water, bring to a boil on the stove, and then turn off. Cover the pot and let sit for an hour or two.

Over a medium heat, bring the beans back to a boil and cook for 20 to 30 minutes. You don't want them to be perfectly soft, more like al dente. Drain off the cooking water.

In a very large roasting pan or casserole dish, combine the semi-cooked beans with the rest of the ingredients and spices and stir thoroughly.

Add enough hot water to the pan or dish so that it just barely comes to the top of the beans. Put a lid on the pan or casserole dish, or cover with tin foil. I cover my roasting pan with tinfoil and then put a lid on it and press down firmly.

Bake the beans at 300°F for 6 hours. They will be tender, aromatic and delectable.

This recipe serves about 8 people. One portion is enough to get you baked.

INGREDIENTS

2 pounds of dry white navy beans, soaked overnight

1/2 cup of Baked Butter (page 13)

1 tablespoon of Worcestershire sauce

1 red onion, chopped

1 green pepper, chopped

1 stalks of celery, chopped

1 cup of frozen corn

2 teaspoons of salt

2 teaspoons of dry mustard

1/2 cup of maple syrup

1/4 cup of brown sugar

1/4 cup of bacon, cut into bite-sized pieces

2 tablespoons of apple cider vinegar

about 2 cups of hot water

Baked Cheese Crescent Rolls

Not your regular French breakfast

Preheat oven to 350°F. Lightly grease a cookie sheet.

Separate the dough into 8 triangles. Drop 2 tablespoons of Chronic Cheese into the middle of each triangle. Roll each into a crescent roll and place, seam down, onto your greased cookie sheet.

Brush each roll with a little of the beaten egg yolk. Bake for 10 to 12 minutes, or until golden brown.

2 to 4 crescent rolls are enough to get you baked.

INGREDIENTS

1 can of refrigerated crescent roll dough

1 cup of Chronic Cheese (page 41)

$1/2$ teaspoon of dried dill

1 egg yolk, beaten

Fried Comfort and Love Sandwich

For those days when you just need a hug

Heat a frying pan over medium heat.

Lightly brush one side of each slice of Burner Bread with the Baked Butter. Place 1 slice of the Burner Bread butter side down into the skillet, and arrange the apple slices evenly over the top. Sprinkle the cheddar cheese over the apple, then top with the remaining slice of Burner Bread, butter-side up.

Fry until the bread is golden brown, then flip the sandwich over. Cook until the other side is golden brown and the cheese has melted. This should take about 1 to 2 more minutes.

One Fried Comfort and Love Sandwich is enough to get you baked.

INGREDIENTS

2 tablespoons of Baked Butter (page 13), melted

2 slices of Burner Bread (page 33)

3 thick slices of pre-cooked bacon

1 Courtland or Northern Spy apple, thinly sliced

2 tablespoons of Mary Jane Mayo (page 53)

2 ounces of Old Cheddar, thinly sliced

Chronic Rarebit Comfort Food

A slice of Wales right on your plate

Melt the Baked Butter in a saucepan over a low heat, then stir in the flour, salt, pepper, mustard, Worcestershire sauce, and hot pepper sauce. Continue cooking and stirring until the mixture is smooth and bubbly. This should take about 5 minutes.

Remove from the heat and gradually stir in the Marijuana Milk.

Return to the heat and stir continually until the mixture comes to a boil. Slowly pour in the cider, and cook for 1 minute more while stirring. Gradually stir in the Chronic Cheese until well combined. Melt the cheddar cheese into the mixture in small portions until completely incorporated. Remove from heat.

Toast both sides of Burner Bread under the broiler until lightly browned.

Divide the cheese mixture evenly between slices and spread to the edges. Return to the broiler until the top is brown and bubbly. This should take 2-3 minutes.

One slice of Chronic Rarebit Comfort Food is enough to get you baked.

INGREDIENTS

1/2 teaspoon of Worcestershire sauce

1 cup of Marijuana Milk made with whole milk (page 27)

1/2 cup of Strongbow or other hard cider

1/2 cup of cheddar cheese, shredded

1/2 cup of Chronic Cheese (page 41)

1/4 cup of Baked Butter (page 13)

1/4 cup of all-purpose flour

1/2 teaspoon of salt

1/4 teaspoon of pepper

1/4 teaspoon of dry mustard

4 thick slices of Burner Bread (page 33)

Karrot Kush Soup

To warm the coldest of hearts

In a soup pot, add the "Oregano" Oil, carrots, onions, and ginger and stir over medium heat until the onions turn translucent. Add the garlic and swirl around just until you can smell it.

Add half the stock to the pot and simmer for about for 3 minutes. Add the remaining stock and bring the soup to a boil for less than a minute. Reduce the heat and let the soup simmer for 5 more minutes. Add the soy sauce and stir.

Add noodles, more vegetables, chicken, or tofu if desired.

This recipe makes 8 servings. 1 bowl of soup is enough to get you baked.

INGREDIENTS

1/3 cup of "Oregano" Oil (page 17)

4 ground cloves of fresh garlic, minced

6 tablespoons of fresh ginger, minced

4 large carrots, peeled and minced

1 or 2 large onions, chopped

8 cups of good chicken stock (vegetable stock if you're vegan)

1/4 cup of soy sauce (or tamari)

Smoked Meat Sandwich Spread

Spice up your lunch!

Combine the Chronic Cheese, mustard, and grated cheese in medium bowl. Mix together. Stir the beef and onion into the cheese mixture.

Refrigerate this mixture for at least an hour before serving. I find it tastes best if you leave it in the fridge overnight before serving.

Spread the mixture evenly on 4 slices of Burner Bread. Spread the other 4 pieces with stone-ground mustard and assemble 4 sandwiches. Serve.

1 sandwich is enough to get you baked.

For extra deliciousness put the sandwiches in a panini press on high for 3 minutes or so, just enough to melt the cheddar.

INGREDIENTS

1 cup of Chronic Cheese (page 41)

1/2 cup of Old White Cheddar, grated finely

1/2 cup of finely chopped smoked beef

1/4 cup of finely chopped green onions

1 teaspoon of Dijon mustard

8 slices of Burner Bread (page 33)

Poetic Pot Sandwich

Smooth like a sonnet

Spread the Chronic Cheese onto one slice of the Burner Bread. Top the cheese with tomato slices, then the Fontina. Top the Fontina with the basil leaves and other slice of bread and press it down a bit to kind of seal the two pieces of bread together.

Butter the outside of the Burner Bread and fry it up like you would with any grilled cheese sandwich. Serve immediately.

1 sandwich is enough to get you baked.

2 slices of thick-sliced Burner Bread (page 33)

3 tablespoons of Chronic Cheese (page 41)

2 ounces of Fontina cheese

1 tablespoon of Baked Butter (page 13)

2 slices of tomato

4 basil leaves

Dinner

Seafood Ragout

The best flavors of the sea

Cut the lobster and sole into 1-inch chunks. Combine the lobster and sole with the shrimp and lemon juice, then set aside.

Heat the "Oregano" Oil in a large stew pot over a medium heat. Add the garlic, celery and onions and cook until translucent. Pour in the tomatoes, vinegar, and wine and let the liquid come to a simmer. Cook for about 10 minutes.

Pour in the fish stock and add the marinated seafood and fish along with the basil, bay leaves, and parsley. Simmer the ragout for about 20 minutes, until the lobster has cooked through.

Season the ragout with salt and pepper to taste.

Serve immediately with crostini. This recipe is enough to get 4 people baked.

INGREDIENTS

1/3 cup of "Oregano" Oil (page 17)

4 ground cloves of garlic, minced

3 stalks of celery, chopped

1 large onion, sliced

1 (15 ounce) can of whole tomatoes

1 cup of balsamic vinegar

1 pound of lobster tails

1 pound of sole fillets

1 pound of medium shrimp, peeled
    and deveined

3 tablespoons of lemon juice

3 cups of Pinot Grigio

5 cups of fish stock

2 bay leaves

3 sprigs of fresh basil leaves, roughly
    torn

4 tablespoons of fresh parsley,
    chopped

sea salt and pepper to taste

Chronic Coconut Chicken

The delicious marriage of poultry and pot

In a medium bowl, mix the cumin, cayenne pepper, turmeric, and coriander. Place the chicken in the bowl, season with salt and pepper, and rub the spice mixture onto all sides.

Heat half the Baked Butter in a wok over a medium heat. Place the chicken in the wok. Cook for 8 to 10 minutes on each side, until the chicken is no longer pink and the juices run clear. Remove the chicken from the wok and set aside.

Heat the remaining Baked Butter in the wok. Cook and stir the onion, ginger, chili paste, and garlic for about 5 minutes, or until the onions are tender.

Add the tomatoes to the wok and continue cooking for 5 to 8 minutes more. Stir in the Marijuana Coconut Milk along with the chicken and juices that were set aside. Allow the chicken and Marijuana Coconut Milk to simmer on medium low heat for another 20 minutes.

Serve immediately and garnish with chopped cilantro. This recipe is enough to get 6 people baked.

INGREDIENTS

1 teaspoon of ground cumin

1 teaspoon of ground cayenne pepper

1 teaspoon of ground turmeric

1 teaspoon of ground coriander

2 teaspoons of chili paste

1 onion, chopped

1 tablespoon of minced fresh ginger

1 bunch of chopped fresh cilantro

2 ground cloves of garlic, minced

3 tomatoes, seeded and chopped

2 cups of Marijuana Coconut Milk (page 27)

4 skinless, boneless chicken breasts

salt and pepper to taste

1/3 cup of Baked Butter (page 13)

Finnan Haddie

A hearty dish with a Scottish soul

In a shallow baking dish, cover the smoked haddock with Marijuana Milk. Let this mixture sit for an hour and a half.

Preheat oven to 350°F. Bake the fish for 30 minutes.

Drain the liquid from the baking dish but make sure you save the liquid. With two forks, separate the fish into flakes.

In a saucepan, melt the Baked Butter over a medium heat. Whisk in the flour until smooth. Gradually stir in the reserved liquid. Cook, stirring constantly, until thickened.

Blend in the eggs. I do this by taking some of the liquid out, mixing it in with the eggs and then pouring the egg mixture into the saucepan.

Add the flaked fish, onions, and potatoes, stirring occasionally, until the fish is warmed up.

Serve in soup bowls. One bowl is enough to get you baked.

INGREDIENTS

1/2 pound of smoked haddock

2 cups of Marijuana Milk (page 27)

1/4 cup of Baked Butter (page 13)

1/3 cup of all-purpose flour

2 eggs, slightly beaten

2 cups of potatoes, cooked and cubed

1 large onion, thinly sliced and sautéed

Crock Pot Goulash

Creamy, full-bodied and perfect for winter

Boil the sausage for 6 minutes in a large pot. Cook the sweet sausage first, and then the spicy sausage. Allow each batch of sausage to cool.

Heat the "Oregano" Oil in a large frying pan over medium heat. Stir in the onion, celery, and garlic and cook until the onion is translucent. This should take about 8 more minutes. Set the frying pan aside.

Pour the mixture into a crock pot. Add the sausage after crumbling it into bite-sized pieces. Put the frying pan back onto the stove over a medium heat. Quickly pour the Chianti into the frying pan and stir to dissolve the brown flavor bits stuck to the bottom of the frying pan.

When the pan bottom is clear, pour the Chianti into the slow cooker. Add the diced tomatoes, tomato sauce, and salt to taste and mix together well. Set the heat on low and cover the crock pot. Let the mixture cook for about 5 hours.

Pour the cream into the sausage mixture, stir, cover, and cook for about 45 more minutes. Check the seasoning one more time before serving. Serve with egg noodles.

This recipe is enough to get 4 people baked.

INGREDIENTS

⅓ cup of "Oregano" Oil (page 17)

1 pound of sweet Italian sausage

1 pound of hot Italian sausage, minced

2 large red onions, diced

6 stalks of celery, diced

5 ground nutmeg of garlic

½ cup of Chianti

1 16-ounce can of diced Roma tomatoes, not drained

1 16-ounce can of tomato sauce

1 cup of heavy cream

sea salt and pepper

Beef with Balsamic Lemon Sauce

Tangy and tasty, this will always impress

Cook slices of tenderloin in the "Oregano" Oil in a frying pan for about 3 minutes on each side. Set the tenderloin on a plate, then make the sauce in the same frying pan.

Mix the stock, balsamic vinegar, pepper, lemon juice, and garlic together in the frying pan. Bring the liquid to a boil and let it reduce a little.

Add the teaspoon of cornstarch and whisk it in. Once the sauce has thickened, whisk in the Baked Butter.

Put the tenderloin back into the frying pan along with any juices that may have escaped, cover, and turn off the heat. Let the meat warm up, and then serve immediately garnished with the parsley.

This recipe is enough to get 4 people baked.

INGREDIENTS

4 slices of beef tenderloin, about an inch thick
1/4 cup of "Oregano" Oil (page 17)
1/2 cup of beef stock
1/3 cup of balsamic vinegar
3 finely ground cloves of garlic
2 tablespoons of Baked Butter (page 13)
1 teaspoon of cornstarch
1/3 cup of fresh chopped parsley
a pinch of pepper
a squeeze of lemon juice

Zesty Lemon Swordfish

A simple dish
with lots of depth!

Preheat the broiler and, if necessary, move a rack to the top of your oven.

In a small bowl, mix the lemon juice with the sea salt until the salt dissolves. Stir in the fresh oregano. Slowly whisk in the "Oregano" Oil and season generously with pepper.

Broil the swordfish steaks under the broiler as close to the heat as possible. Broil for about 3 minutes until you get a nice color. Turn the steaks over and broil the other side for another 3 minutes or so until you get a nice color on that side as well.

Transfer the fish to a platter with a rim on it. Pierce each fish steak in several places with a fork to allow the sauce to penetrate.

Beat the sauce one last time before drizzling it over the fish. Serve at once.

Serve with crostini. This recipe is enough to get 4 people baked.

INGREDIENTS

⅓ cup of "Oregano" Oil (page 17)

4 swordfish steaks (about 2 pounds)

¼ cup of fresh lemon juice

4 teaspoons of fresh oregano, chopped

sea salt and freshly ground pepper

Spaghetti Marinara

Just like Mama used to make!

Sauté the sliced onions and garlic in the olive oil over medium heat for about 3 minutes or until they're soft. Add the can of tomatoes, turn up the heat, and cook quickly for 3 minutes. Lower the heat at that point and let the sauce simmer for about an hour.

Chop the anchovies and add them to the sauce along with cracked black pepper, a small pinch of sea salt, and the sugar. Allow to simmer for another 10 minutes then add the oregano. Keep warm over a low heat until ready to serve.

Cook the spaghetti in salted water until tender. Drain and serve in a large, heated platter (with preheated individual plates on the side). Pour marinara sauce over the spaghetti and sprinkle the grated Romano cheese over the top.

Serve immediately or divide the sauce into 4 servings. This recipe is enough to get 4 people baked.

INGREDIENTS

1 pound of spaghetti

28-ounce can of plum tomatoes

1/3 cup of "Oregano" Oil (page 17)

2 onions, sliced

2 ground cloves of minced garlic

2 filets of anchovies

1/4 teaspoon of sugar

1/4 cup of grated Romano cheese

1 teaspoon of dried oregano

sea salt and cracked black pepper

Mediterranean Chicken Schnitzel

Your new favorite weeknight dinner

Season the chicken with salt and pepper. Put the flour in a bag and then add the chicken. Shake the chicken around while inside the bag so the breasts are dredged with flour. Take the chicken out and shake off the excess flour. Set the chicken aside.

In a large, deep frying pan melt 2 tablespoons of the Baked Butter with 3 tablespoons of the "Oregano" Oil over medium high heat. When the butter and oil start to sizzle, add 2 pieces of the chicken at a time and cook for 2 to 3 minutes until browned.

Turn the chicken over and cook the other side for another 2-3 minutes. Remove from the frying pan and transfer to plate.

Melt 2 more tablespoons of Baked Butter and add 2 tablespoons "Oregano" Oil together. When butter and oil start to sizzle, repeat the same process as above with the other 2 pieces of chicken. When they're browned on both sides, transfer them to the plate, as well.

Add the lemon juice, the capers, and the chicken stock to the same pan. Bring this sauce to a boil while scraping down brown bits from the sides and bottom of the pan. Add the fried chicken to the sauce in the frying pan. Bring the temperature up on the chicken by simmering the breasts for about 5 minutes.

INGREDIENTS

- 1/3 cup of Baked Butter
- 1/4 cup of "Oregano" Oil (page 17)
- 1/2 cup of fresh lemon juice
- 1/2 cup of chicken stock
- 1/3 cup of capers
- 1/4 cup of fresh parsley, chopped
- 2 skinless and boneless chicken breasts, cut in half and pounded (not too thin)
- all-purpose flour, for dredging
- sea salt and freshly ground black pepper

Arrange the chicken on a platter. Add the rest of the remaining Baked Butter to the sauce and whisk briskly. Pour the sauce over the chicken and garnish with the chopped parsley.

Serve immediately. This recipe is enough to get 4 people baked.

Vegetarian

Vestige Verde Sauce
Salsa into summer with this deliciousness

Put all of the ingredients in a blender or food processor, and blend until the sauce is smooth and velvety.

When the sauce is velvety smooth, pour directly over the steamed vegetables, lentil loaf or pan-seared seitan.

There are 4 servings of sauce in this recipe.

1 serving of the Vestige Verde Sauce is enough to get you baked.

INGREDIENTS

1 cup of Chronic Cheese (page 41)

1 large clove of garlic, finely minced

1/2 cup (or more depending on your preference) of fresh cilantro leaves, ripped off the stems

1 tablespoon of fresh lime juice

1/4 cup of Baked Yogurt (page 43)

1 cup of salsa verde

1 teaspoon of freshly ground black pepper

1 teaspoon of sea salt

1/2 teaspoon of ground cumin

Zucchini and Tomato Gratin

A blend of beautiful cheeses makes this vegetable dish come to life

Preheat oven to 375°F. Move an oven rack into the top third of the oven.

Heat the "Oregano" Oil in a large frying pan over medium heat, and spread the zucchini slices into the pan in a single layer. If they don't fit you will have to cook them in batches, or use two frying pans, otherwise the zucchini will get mushy.

Sprinkle the crushed garlic over the zucchini and cook until the slices are golden brown on both sides, about 8 minutes per side. Remove them from the frying pan.

Arrange the slices of zucchini in a 9 x 12-inch glass baking dish. Build up layers in the pan by alternating the zucchini with slices of mozzarella and slices of tomato, so that the slices overlap each other in a neat pattern of rows. Sprinkle the Parmesan and basil over the top layer of the dish, and season to taste with salt and pepper.

Bake in the preheated oven until the cheese is melted and brown and the dish is bubbling. This should take about 30 minutes. This recipe is enough to get 4 people baked.

INGREDIENTS

- ⅓ cup of "Oregano" Oil (page 17)
- 6 zucchini, sliced
- 2 large cloves of garlic, crushed
- 8 ounces of mozzarella, sliced thinly
- 6 large tomatoes, peeled and sliced
- ½ cup of Parmesan, grated
- 3 tablespoons of fresh basil, chopped
- sea salt and freshly ground black pepper

Penne with Mandorla Sauce

Sweet and nutty accents make this
not your usual tomato sauce

Heat the "Oregano" Oil in a medium saucepan over medium heat. Add the garlic and cook until it is a light golden brown in color, which should take less than 2 minutes. Add the almonds to the saucepan and cook them for another 2 minutes or until they are lightly golden brown.

Cook the penne in sea-salted water until tender. Drain.

In a food processor or blender place the almonds and peppers and combine with the broth, tomato paste, parsley, vinegar, salt, sugar, and pepper. Blend until the mixture is pureed. Transfer to a large heated serving bowl.

Toss the hot, drained penne with the sauce. Serve hot, warm, or room temperature. Serve immediately or divide the sauce into 4 servings. This recipe is enough to get 4 people baked.

INGREDIENTS

1 pound of penne pasta

1/3 cup of "Oregano" Oil (page 17)

4 cloves of garlic, minced

1/2 cup of almonds, slivered

2 cups of roasted red peppers

1/2 cup of vegetable broth

3 tablespoons of tomato paste

1 tablespoon of red wine vinegar

1/4 cup of fresh parsley, chopped

1/2 teaspoon of sugar

sea salt and cracked black pepper
to taste

Pot Peanut Soup

Because peanut butter
goes with everything

In a 6 quart crock pot or larger, combine the vegetable stock, celery, salt, onion, garlic, Oregano Oil, chili paste, and Pot Peanut Butter.

Cover and cook on high for 2 to 3 hours.

Whisk together the Marijuana Coconut Milk, all-purpose flour and water until smooth.

Add to crock pot. Cover and cook on high for an additional 20 minutes, stirring occasionally. Garnish individual servings with chopped peanuts and cilantro. I like to serve a slice of lime on the side as well.

Serve in warmed bowls with some naan. Half a cup is enough to get you baked.

INGREDIENTS

6 cups of vegetable stock

1/2 cup of celery, finely chopped

1/2 teaspoon of salt

1 medium onion, finely chopped

1 teaspoon of Sambal Oelek (fresh ground chili paste)

2 cloves of fresh garlic, minced

4 tablespoons of "Oregano" Oil (page 17)

1 cup of Pot Peanut Butter (page 13)

2 cups of Marijuana Coconut Milk (page 27)

1/2 cup of all-purpose flour

1/2 cup of water

1/2 cup of peanuts, finely chopped

1/2 cup of chopped fresh cilantro or parsley

Harvest Ratatouille

Healthy, decadent, and absolutely beautiful

Preheat oven to 375°F. Lightly grease a large loaf pan or casserole dish.

Melt the syrup and the Baked Butter together in a saucepan over low heat.

In a loaf pan, layer the vegetables in a decorative fashion, pouring a little Marijuana Milk over the top, then the Baked Butter syrup, then sprinkle with salt and pepper and a little of the grated cheeses in between each layer.

Layer like lasagna. Fill the loaf pan in this manner, and then bake for 30 minutes.

Turn out and serve. Garnish with a dusting of Parmesan if you'd like. Serve immediately.

To make this a vegan recipe, substitute the Baked Butter for "Oregano" Oil, use Marijuana Coconut Milk, and sprinkle with ground cashews instead of cheese.

This recipe is enough to get 4 people baked.

INGREDIENTS

2 cups of sliced cauliflower, cooked until slightly tender, then cooled

1 cup of sliced carrots, cooked until slightly tender, then cooled

1 cup of sliced parsnips, cooked until slightly tender, then cooled

1 cup of sliced onion, cooked until slightly tender, then cooled

1 cup of sliced sweet potato, cooked until slightly tender, then cooled

1 bunch of kale, roughly chopped

a pinch of ground nutmeg

3 tablespoons of Baked Butter (page 13)

1 tablespoon of pure maple syrup

1/2 cup of Marijuana Milk (page 27)

1/2 cup of Parmesan

1/2 cup of mozzarella

sea salt and black pepper, to taste

Baked Tomatoes with Lentils

A hot and hearty dish
for a cold winter's night

Preheat the broiler.

Remove the cores from each tomato.

Mix the breadcrumbs, crushed basil, Burner Bread crumbs, Baked Yogurt, lentils, and Romano cheese together and stuff into the tomatoes.

Arrange the tomatoes in a foil pie pan. Broil the tomatoes for 10 minutes, or until the filling is golden brown.

Arrange each tomato on its own plate. Sprinkle each tomato with fresh basil and splash a tablespoon of the "Oregano" Oil over each tomato.

Serve immediately. One tomato is enough to get you baked.

INGREDIENTS

½ cup of cooked lentils

4 medium tomatoes

3 tablespoons of Baked Yogurt
(page 43)

1 teaspoon dried basil, crushed

2 tablespoons of Burner Bread
crumbs (page 33)

2 tablespoons of Romano cheese,
grated

4 tablespoons of "Oregano Oil"
(page 17)

"Oregano" Oil (for garnish)

basil leaves (for garnish)

Cheesy Cauliflower Bean Bake

A decadent dish that's rich and delicious

Preheat oven to 400°F. Grease a glass baking dish with a little Baked Butter.

Place the cauliflower and navy beans in prepared dish.

In a small bowl, stir together the Parmesan, breadcrumbs, 2 tablespoons of the melted Baked Butter and the parsley until well mixed. Sprinkle over cauliflower, tossing gently.

Bake for 15 minutes or until lightly browned and heated through. Remove from the oven.

Transfer cauliflower to a serving dish and drizzle with remaining melted Baked Butter.

Serve immediately with crostini. This recipe is enough to get 4 people baked.

INGREDIENTS

1 can of white navy beans, drained

1 head of cauliflower, slightly cooked, cooled and broken into florets

1/2 cup of grated Parmesan

1/2 cup of Burner Bread crumbs (page 33)

1/2 cup of Baked Butter (page 13), melted

1 teaspoon of dried parsley

 Vegetarian

Stuffed Peppers

They're stuffed.

You'll be loaded

Preheat the oven to 375°F.

Heat 1 tablespoon of the "Oregano" Oil in a medium frying pan over moderate heat. Add the onion and sauté until soft and sweet, after about 5 minutes. Set aside.

In a mixing bowl combine the onion, Burner Bread crumbs, tomato, cheese, almonds, mint, and 2 tablespoons of "Oregano" Oil. Stir well, then season with salt and pepper.

Arrange the peppers so that they are standing up with the open end facing up in a shallow, oiled baking dish. Fill each pepper with the bread-crumb mixture equally. Drizzle with the remaining "Oregano" Oil.

Bake until well browned and crisp on top. This should take about 30 minutes.

Serve warm or at room temperature, but not hot. This recipe is enough to get 4 people baked.

INGREDIENTS

4 tablespoons of "Oregano" Oil
(page 17)

1 small onion, minced

3/4 cup of Burner Bread crumbs
(page 33)

1/2 cup of finely chopped tomato

1/2 cup of freshly grated Parmesan

2 tablespoons of chopped fresh mint

1/2 cup of slivered almonds

4 large red bell peppers, seeded

sea salt and freshly ground pepper
to taste

Desserts

Bars and Squares

French-Canadian Sugar Squares

A maple syrupy homage
to French Canadian Sugar Pie

Grease a 9 x 9-inch square pan. Preheat oven to 350°F.

Cut 1/2 cup of Baked Butter into 1 cup of the flour with the sugar. Press the mixture into the square pan. Bake this crust for 15 minutes.

Combine the cream, egg, and remaining flour with the remaining Baked Butter, maple syrup, and brown sugar. Pour this mixture into the crust and return the pan to the oven.

Bake for another 25 to 30 minutes or until the mixture swells. Cool thoroughly before cutting into 20 squares. 1 or 2 squares is enough to get you baked.

INGREDIENTS

- 1/2 cup + 2 tablespoons of Baked Butter (page 13)
- 1 cup + 1 tablespoon of all-purpose flour
- 2 tablespoons of sugar
- 1/4 cup of heavy cream (or soya cream/coconut milk)
- 1 egg
- 1 cup of maple syrup
- 1 cup of brown sugar

Scottish Brownies
A shortbread crust for a
mind-meltingly delicious treat

Preheat the oven to 300°F.

In a medium bowl, stir together the rice flour and sugar. Cut in the Baked Butter until the mixture is crumbly. Press the mixture firmly into the bottom of a 9 x 9-inch baking pan.

Bake for 20 to 25 minutes until firm and only ever-so-slightly golden. Set aside to cool.

Preheat the oven to 350°F.

In a medium sized mixing bowl, mix together the all-purpose flour, baking powder, and cocoa powder. Make a well in the center of these ingredients, and add the egg, vanilla, and sweetened condensed milk. Mix this batter until it is well combined. Stir in the chocolate chips and the pecans if you choose to use them. Spread the mixture over the cooled crust.

Bake for 20 minutes in the preheated oven, until the brownies begin to pull away from the edges and the top appears dry.

Cool thoroughly and cut into squares. Store tightly covered at room temperature. One brownie is enough to get you baked.

INGREDIENTS

1 cup of rice flour

1/4 cup of white sugar

1/2 cup of softened Baked Butter (page 13)

1/4 cup of all-purpose flour

1/4 cup of unsweetened cocoa powder

1/2 teaspoon of baking powder

1 egg

1 1/2 teaspoons of pure vanilla extract

1 (14-ounce) can of sweetened condensed milk

1 cup of chocolate chips

3/4 cup of chopped pecans (optional)

New Old-Fashioned Squares

A fresh twist on a classic

Preheat oven to 350°F. Grease a 12 x 12-inch square pan.

Cream the Baked Butter with an electric hand mixer until fluffy. Add in the sugar and eggs and beat well. This should take about 2 minutes.

With a spoon, stir in the melted chocolate, flour, nuts, and salt until the batter is an even color.

Pour the batter into the prepared baking pan. Bake for 20 to 25 minutes.

Cool thoroughly before cutting into 24 squares. 1 square is enough to get you baked.

INGREDIENTS

$^1/_2$ cup of Baked Butter (page 13)

$1^3/_4$ cups of brown sugar

2 eggs

$^3/_4$ cup of melted chocolate

1 cup of almonds

1 cup of cashews

1 cup of pecans

$1^1/_2$ cups of flour

$^1/_2$ teaspoon of salt

Captain Morgan Blondies

Enough rum to make even
the fiercest pirate smile

Preheat oven to 350°F. Grease a 9 x 9-inch baking dish; glass works best.

Sift together the flour, spices, sugar, and salt. Set aside.

In a large mixing bowl, beat together the Baked Butter and eggs until creamy. Beat in the milk as well as the rum.

Gradually stir the flour mixture into the egg mixture. Stir in the chips and nuts.

Pour the batter into the prepared baking dish. Bake for 30 minutes or until the blondies start begin to pull away from the edges and the top appears dry.

Cool thoroughly and cut into squares. Store tightly covered at room temperature.

1 blondie is enough to get you baked.

INGREDIENTS

1 1/2 cups of all-purpose flour

1 teaspoon of ground cinnamon

1 teaspoon of ground ginger

1/2 teaspoon of ground nutmeg

1/4 teaspoon of ground allspice

3/4 cup of sugar

a pinch of salt

2/3 cup of Baked Butter (page 13)

3 large eggs

1/4 cup of milk

3 tablespoons of rum

2/3 cup of butterscotch chips

1/2 cup of chopped nuts (use your
   favorite)

Crack

So good they're dangerously addictive

These bars are affectionately called "Crack" because on more than one occasion I found myself eating more than the desired amount because they taste so good. I've become addicted to them. Be extra careful with any of the desserts you find yourself addicted to.

Preheat oven to 350°F. Grease a 9 x 9-inch baking dish; glass works best.

Mix all ingredients together in a bowl. When thoroughly combined, pour into the baking dish.

Bake at 375°F for about 8 to 10 minutes or until it looks golden-brown and bubbly. When they're done, take them out of the oven and pull the crack away from all four sides.

Allow to cool for 5 minutes, and then cut into squares. Loosen the edges again and allow them to cool thoroughly before removing the squares from the pan.

1 square of Crack is enough to get you baked.

INGREDIENTS

2 cups of instant oats

1 cup of packed brown sugar

1/2 cup of Baked Butter (page 13), melted

1/2 teaspoon of pure vanilla extract

Dreamy Raspberry Bars

Three layers of dreamy,
jammy goodness.

Preheat oven to 375°F.

Combine the Baked Butter, flour, baking soda, brown sugar, milk, egg yolks, and 1/4 cup of white sugar together to form a dough. Press into a 9 x 9-inch pan. Bake for 12 minutes until the edges are lightly golden brown.

When you remove the base from the oven, spread the raspberry jam evenly across it. Set the pan aside.

Bring the oven down to 350°F.

Beat the egg whites with an electric hand mixer until they form stiff peaks. Fold the cup of white sugar, butter, vanilla, and nuts gently into the egg whites until combined. Pour over the raspberry jam.

Bake for 20 to 25 minutes or until golden brown. Allow to cool thoroughly before cutting into 12 squares. 1 square is enough to get you baked.

INGREDIENTS

1/2 cup of Baked Butter (page 13)

1 1/2 cups of flour

1 teaspoon of baking soda

1/4 cup of brown sugar

1 cup + 1/4 cup of white sugar

1 tablespoon of milk

1 egg

1/2 cup of really good raspberry jam

2 tablespoons of butter

2 eggs, separated

1/4 teaspoon of salt

1 teaspoon of pure vanilla extract

1 cup of chopped pecans

Desserts

Cookies

Chocolate Chip Cookies

Not like grandma used to make

Preheat oven to 300°F.

Cream the Baked Butter with both of the sugars, using an electric mixer on medium speed, until fluffy. This should take 30 seconds.

Beat in the egg and the vanilla extract for another 30 seconds.

In a mixing bowl or on wax paper, sift together the flour, baking soda, baking powder, and salt 3 times and beat into the butter mixture at low speed for about 15 seconds. Stir in the chocolate chips.

Using an ice-cream scoop or a serving spoon, drop the cookie dough (about 2 tablespoons of dough works best) onto a greased cookie sheet. Gently press down on the dough to spread out the cookie into a 2-inch circle. Repeat, keeping the cookies 2¹/₂ inches apart.

Bake for about 18 minutes or until nicely browned around the edges. Bake the cookies a little longer for crunchier cookies. 2 Chocolate Chip Cookies are enough to get you baked.

INGREDIENTS

- ¹/₂ cup of Baked Butter (page 13), softened
- 1 cup of light brown sugar
- 3 tablespoons of granulated sugar
- 1 large egg
- 2 teaspoons of pure vanilla extract
- 1³/₄ cups of all-purpose flour
- ¹/₂ teaspoon of baking powder
- ¹/₂ teaspoon of baking soda
- ¹/₂ teaspoon of salt
- 1¹/₂ cups of semi-sweet chocolate chips

Double Chocolate Delights

Indulge the chocolate addict in your life!

Cream the Baked Butter with an electric hand mixer in a medium sized bowl. Add the melted chocolate, then the sugar, then the eggs. Beat until thoroughly combined. Set aside.

In another bowl or on waxed paper, combine the flour, cocoa, baking powder, and salt. Sift these ingredients together 3 times.

Fold the dry ingredients into the butter mixture, alternating with the chocolate milk. Add the vanilla extract. Cover the bowl with Saran Wrap and refrigerate for 3 hours.

Preheat oven to 400°F.

Roll the dough into a log shape then cut slices about 1/4 inch thick. Place the slices, 1 1/2 inches apart, on a large, ungreased cookie sheet. Bake for 10 minutes.

Remove from the oven and let cool. 2 cookies are enough to get you baked.

INGREDIENTS

1/2 cup of Baked Butter (page 13)

1 cup of sugar

1/4 cup of melted chocolate

1 egg

1/3 cup of chocolate milk (or chocolate soya milk)

1 teaspoon of pure vanilla extract

2 cups of flour

1 tablespoon of cocoa

1 1/2 teaspoons of baking powder

a pinch of salt

Fresh Fragrant Fancies

Best enjoyed with a steaming cup of mint tea

In a medium bowl, cream together the Baked Butter, white sugar, and icing sugar until the mixture is light and fluffy. Mix in the lavender, mint, and lemon zest.

Combine the flour, cornstarch, and salt. Mix these into the batter until well blended.

Divide the dough into 2 balls, wrap them separately in plastic wrap, and flatten the balls to a 1-inch thickness. Refrigerate the dough until firm. This should take about an hour.

Preheat the oven to 325°F.

On a lightly floured surface, roll the dough out to 1/4-inch thickness. Cut into shapes with cookie cutters. Cookie stamps will work well on these too if you're feeling extra creative and so inclined. Place the cookies on cookie sheets.

Bake for 18 to 20 minutes, just until the cookies begin to brown at the edges. Cool for a few minutes on the baking sheets then transfer to wire racks to cool the cookies completely. 2 to 3 cookies are enough to get you baked.

INGREDIENTS

- 3/4 cup of oil
- 1/2 cup of Baked Butter, (page 13), softened
- 2/3 cup of white sugar
- 1/4 cup of icing sugar, sifted
- 2 tablespoons of fresh lavender, finely chopped
- 2 teaspoons of fresh mint, chopped
- 1 teaspoon of lemon zest, grated
- 2 1/2 cups of all-purpose flour
- 1/2 cup of cornstarch
- a pinch of salt

Peanut Butter Cup Cookies

So good they need a warning label

Preheat oven to 375°F.

Sift together the flour, salt, and baking soda on a piece of waxed paper or in a bowl and set aside.

Cream together the Baked Butter, sugar, peanut butter, and brown sugar until fluffy. Beat in the egg, vanilla, and cream and blend the mixture together until it's all combined. Add the flour mixture a little at a time. Mix it thoroughly.

Shape the dough into 24 balls and place each ball into one cup of an ungreased mini muffin pan. Bake for 8 to 10 minutes.

Remove from oven and immediately press a mini peanut butter cup into each ball. Do this as fast as you can.

Cool the cups before you carefully remove them from the baking pan. I use a butter knife to lift the cup out, much like I would a mini muffin.

1 cup should be enough to get you baked. If it isn't, then split a cup in half, eat one half and then wait at least 30 minutes before eating the other half.

INGREDIENTS

- 3/4 cup of packed brown sugar
- 1/4 cup of white sugar
- 1/2 cup of peanut butter
- 1/2 cup of Baked Butter (page 13), softened
- 1 lightly beaten egg
- 2 tablespoons of 10% cream (or soy cream)
- 1 teaspoon of pure vanilla extract
- 1 3/4 cups of all-purpose flour
- 1 teaspoon of baking soda
- 1/2 teaspoon of salt
- 24 miniature peanut butter cups

White Queen Cookies
A recipe fit for royalty

Preheat the oven 350°F.

In a medium bowl, mix together the Baked Butter, sugar, and lavender until smooth. Add the egg, milk, and vanilla.

In another bowl, mix the oatmeal, flour, and baking powder together. Add in the chocolate chips.

Mix the butter mixture and oatmeal mixture together to form a soft dough.

Drop one spoonful of the cookie dough onto a very lightly greased or nonstick cookie sheet. Repeat, leaving 2 inches between cookies.

Bake for about 8 to 10 minutes.

Allow the cookies to cool before consuming. 2 cookies are enough to get you baked.

For a little variation you can also add chopped, blanched almonds or shredded coconut. Use about half a cup of each.

INGREDIENTS

- 1/2 cup of Baked Butter (page 13)
- 1/2 cup of brown sugar
- 1 1/2 tablespoons of culinary grade lavender flowers
- 1 egg
- 2 1/4 tablespoons of milk
- 1 teaspoon of pure vanilla extract
- 1 cup of oatmeal
- 1 1/2 cups of flour
- 3/4 teaspoon of baking powder
- 1 cup of white chocolate chips

Mint Chocolate Bundles

Melty, minty, marvelous

In a large pan over low heat, melt the Baked Butter, sugar, and water. Add the chocolate chips and stir until only partially melted. Remove the pan from the heat and continue to stir until the chocolate is completely melted. Pour into a large bowl and let cool for 10 minutes.

With a hand mixer at high speed, beat the eggs, 1 at a time, into the chocolate mixture. Reduce the speed of the mixer to low and add the flour, baking soda, and salt, beating until blended.

Cover the dough in Saran Wrap. Chill the dough for an hour and a half in the fridge.

Preheat oven to 350°F.

Roll the dough into balls and place them on an ungreased cookie sheet about 2 inches apart. Ever so lightly and gently smack the top of the ball to create a flat surface. Bake for 8 to 10 minutes.

As soon as the cookies are brought out of the oven, put one chocolate-covered mint on top of each cookie. Let the mint sit for about 5 minutes until melted, then spread the melted mint on top of the cookie.

2 Mint Chocolate Bundles are enough to get you baked.

INGREDIENTS

3/4 cup of packed brown sugar

3/4 cup of white sugar

3/4 cup of Baked Butter (page 13)

2 tablespoons of carbonated water (I use Perrier)

2 eggs

2 1/2 cups of all-purpose flour

1 1/4 teaspoons of baking soda

1/2 teaspoon of salt

2 cups of chocolate chips

40 chocolate-covered mints

Peanut Butter Cookies

Smooth or crunchy? The choice is yours!

Preheat oven to 325°F. Lightly grease a cookie sheet.

Cream the Baked Butter, peanut butter, and both of the sugars together. Blend the egg into the sugar mixture and set aside.

In a separate bowl or on wax paper combine the flour, soda, and salt. Sift together three times.

Stir the flour mixture into the sugar mixture and combine thoroughly. Roll the mixture into 1-inch balls. Place the balls about an inch apart on a cookie sheet and press the tines of a fork into each ball to flatten.

Bake for 12 to 15 minutes. Allow to cool.

2 Peanut Butter Cookies are enough to get you baked.

INGREDIENTS

$1/2$ cup of peanut butter
$1/2$ cup of Baked Butter (page 13)
$1/2$ cup of white sugar
$1/2$ cup of brown sugar
1 egg
$1 1/2$ cups of flour
1 teaspoon of baking soda
a pinch of salt

Lavender Love Bites

A tender herby kiss

Preheat oven to 350°F. Grease a cookie sheet.

Cream together the Baked Butter and sugar. Beat the egg, then blend it into the butter mixture. Mix in the lavender flowers and the flour. Drop the dough, a teaspoonful at a time, onto a cookie sheet.

Bake 15 to 20 minutes, or until golden. Remove the cookies to cooling racks so that the underside of the cookie doesn't get soggy.

2 Lavender Love Bites are enough to get you baked.

INGREDIENTS

^{1}/$_2$ cup of Baked Butter (page 13)

^{1}/$_2$ cup of sugar

1 egg

2 teaspoons of lavender flowers

1^1/$_2$ cups of all-purpose flour

Pumpkin Ice Cream

Because you can't have cookies without it

In a bowl, whisk together the pumpkin puree and vanilla. Cover and refrigerate for at least 3 hours.

Combine the Marijuana Coconut Milk and heavy whipping cream into a saucepan along with the sugar. Bring to 170°F to dissolve sugar then let cool at room temperature.

Grate the nutmeg into the pumpkin mixture and add the other spices. Chill both mixtures overnight in the refrigerator.

The next day, add a little of the milk mixture into the pumpkin mixture and combine well, to loosen it up. Continue mixing them together a little at a time, until totally combined.

Transfer the mixture to an ice-cream maker and freeze according to the manufacturer's instructions. Add the Baked Bourbon during the last minute of churning. Transfer the ice cream to a freezer-safe container. Cover and freeze until firm, at least 3 hours or up to 3 days, before serving. Makes about 1 quart.

This recipe is enough to get 6 people baked.

4 cups of Marijuana Coconut Milk (page 27)

2 cups of heavy whipping cream

1 teaspoon of pure vanilla extract

1 1/2 cups of white sugar

1/2 cup of light brown sugar

1 cup of fresh pumpkin puree or canned, unsweetened pumpkin puree

1 teaspoon of nutmeg, freshly grated

1 teaspoon of ground cinnamon

1/2 teaspoon of ground ginger

1/4 teaspoon of ground cloves

2 tablespoons of Baked Bourbon made via the Alcohol Extraction method (page 29)

Desserts

Cakes

Aloha Hawaiian Bread

A little taste of the islands

Preheat the oven to 350°F. Line the bottom of a well-greased loaf pan with waxed paper.

In small bowl, thoroughly smash bananas and set aside.

In another bowl, cream together the sugar, shortening, and Baked Butter. Add the smashed bananas and eggs. Mix well.

On a piece of waxed paper or in a bowl, combine the flour, baking powder, and salt. Sift together three times.

Add the flour mixture into the banana mixture and stir until the flour is moistened. Pour into the prepared loaf pan. Drop the loaf pan gently onto the countertop three or four times to remove any air bubbles.

Bake for 1 hour, or until a toothpick inserted near the center comes out clean. When cooled thoroughly, cut into 12 slices.

1 slice of Aloha Hawaiian Bread is enough to get you baked.

INGREDIENTS

3/4 cup of macadamia nuts, coarsely chopped

1/2 cup of dark brown sugar

1/2 cup of Baked Butter (page 13)

1/2 cup of shortening

3/4 cup of brown sugar

1/4 cup of white sugar

1 egg

1 cup of smashed banana

1 1/4 cups of pastry flour

1/2 teaspoon of baking powder

a pinch of salt

Banana Cream Cake

A grown-up take on a childhood classic

Grease and flour a 9-inch spring form pan. Preheat the oven to 350°F.

With a hand mixer beat the Baked Butter and sugar together until it's very fluffy and then beat it for about 2 minutes longer. Add one egg at a time and beat the mixture back to the fluffy consistency after each one.

Add in the smashed banana, then the liqueur, and mix thoroughly. Set aside.

In another bowl or on a sheet of waxed paper combine the flour, baking powder, baking soda, and salt. Sift together 3 times. Once sifted, add the flour mixture to the banana mixture a third at a time and make sure it's well combined.

Pour the batter into the pan. Gently drop the pan onto a counter or flat surface about three times to remove the air bubbles.

Bake for 40 minutes, or until a toothpick inserted near the center comes out clean. When cooled thoroughly, ice the cake if you have a sweet tooth (recipe follows). If you don't then don't bother with the icing.

Cut into 12 slices. 1 slice of Banana Cream Cake is enough to get you baked.

INGREDIENTS

½ cup of Baked Butter (page 13)

2 eggs

1 cup of smashed bananas

⅔ cup of sugar

¼ cup of Irish Cream liqueur

2 cups + 2 tablespoons of flour

1 teaspoon of baking powder

1 teaspoon of baking soda

a pinch of salt

Banana Cream Cake

INGREDIENTS

¹/₂ cup of Baked Butter (page 13)

3 cups of icing sugar

¹/₄ cup of Irish Cream liqueur

¹/₃ cup of melted chocolate chips

BANANA CREAM ICING

With an electric hand mixer, cream the Baked Butter until fluffy.

Blend in the melted chocolate and icing sugar alternately with the Irish Cream.

Beat on high until your desired consistency is achieved. If it's too dry, add more Irish Cream. If it's too wet add more icing sugar.

Ice the Banana Cream Cake and serve. Be extra careful, as the iced cake will contain a double whammy of pot: Baked Butter in the cake as well as the icing.

The Devil's Manna

A satanically good chocolate cake

Preheat the oven to 350°F. Grease and flour two 8-inch cake pans.

Combine the cocoa, baking soda, and salt together in a bowl or on waxed paper. Sift together 3 times and set aside.

In a medium bowl, cream the Baked Butter and sugar together with an electric hand mixer until fluffy. Add the eggs one at a time until well blended. Add the melted chocolate until the color of the batter is consistent.

Fold in the a third of the flour mixture at a time, alternating with a third of the buttermilk. Take your time, as it's important to get all the ingredients incorporated well.

Pour the batter evenly into both pans. Gently drop the pans onto a counter or flat surface three times, to remove the air bubbles.

Bake for 35 to 40 minutes, or until a toothpick inserted near the center comes out clean. Let cool and ice with any kind of icing you like (maybe even Banana Icing). Cut into 12 slices.

1 slice is enough to get you baked.

INGREDIENTS

½ cup of Baked Butter (page 13)

2 eggs

½ cup of melted chocolate

1 cup of buttermilk (or vegan substitute, follows)

2 cups of cake flour

1 teaspoon of baking soda

2 tablespoons of cocoa

¼ teaspoon of salt

VEGAN SUBSTITUTE FOR 1 CUP OF BUTTERMILK

¼ cup of silken tofu

½ cup + 3 tablespoons of water

1 tablespoon of lemon juice or vinegar

a pinch of salt

Sour Cream Cake

A crusty, crumby treat with a tang

Preheat oven to 350°F. Grease a 9 x 9-inch inch baking pan.

Combine the Baked Butter, brown sugar, and corn syrup. Spread out evenly on the bottom of the prepared baking dish. Sprinkle the chopped nuts over the mixture in the pan.

Combine the cake mix, eggs, sour cream, and water in a large mixing bowl. With an electric hand mixer beat the mixture for 4 to 5 minutes at a medium speed until the batter is smooth. Pour the batter into the baking pan over top of the nuts.

Bake for 50 minutes or until a toothpick inserted near the center comes out clean. Let cool for 2 minutes then loosen the edges of the cake from the side of the pan. Put your serving plate on top of the cake pan, upside down, then flip the whole thing. The cake should pop right onto the plate.

Allow the cake to cool for 5 more minutes. Cut into 20 pieces. 1 piece is enough to get you baked.

½ cup of Baked Butter (page 13)

2 tablespoons of light corn syrup

½ cup of brown sugar

½ cup of chopped almonds

1 box of white or golden cake mix

2 eggs

1 cup of sour cream

¼ cup of water

Vienna Bundt Cake

Because it's too hard
to pronounce Marmorgugelhupf

Preheat oven to 350°F. Generously grease and flour a bundt cake pan.

Mix the Baked Butter, sugar, flour, cinnamon, instant coffee granules and chopped nuts together until crumbly, then set aside.

Combine the cake mix, water, oil, and eggs and beat with an electric hand mixer on low speed until it all comes together. Beat the mixture on a medium speed for another 4 minutes.

Pour ⅓ of the batter into the prepared bundt pan then sprinkle with ½ of the crumby mixture as evenly as possible. Repeat, then finish with the last ⅓ of the batter on top.

Bake for 50 minutes or until a toothpick inserted near the center comes out clean. Allow the cake to cool for 10 minutes then loosen the edges of the cake from the side of the pan. Put your serving plate on top of the cake pan, upside down, then flip the whole thing. The cake should pop right onto the plate. Let cool completely.

If desired, you can sprinkle the top with icing sugar, or mix 1 teaspoon of hot water into a cup of icing sugar and drizzle the glaze over the top of the bundt cake, allowing it to dribble down the sides. Cut into 16 slices. 1 slice is enough to get you baked.

INGREDIENTS

½ cup of Baked Butter (page 13)

½ cup of flour

1 cup of brown sugar

2 teaspoons of ground cinnamon

½ teaspoon of instant coffee (or instant cappuccino)

½ cup of chopped almonds

1 box of devil's food cake mix

1 cup of water

3 eggs

¼ cup of canola oil

Cinderella Cake with Princess Icing

Cindy, you *shall* go to the ball! And you'll be high!

Preheat oven to 350°F. Grease and flour two 9-inch round layer cake pans.

Combine the sugar, Cannabis Coconut Oil and eggs in a large bowl. Mix well.

Sift the flour, baking soda, cinnamon, ginger, baking powder, and salt into a separate bowl. Stir into the oil mixture, beating well. Stir in pumpkin puree.

Pour the batter into the pans. Bake for 35 to 40 minutes. Turn out onto racks to cool.

When cooled thoroughly, ice the cake if you have a sweet tooth (recipe follows). If you don't then don't bother with the icing.

INGREDIENTS

2 cups of sugar

1 cup of Cannabis Coconut Oil
  (page 21)

4 large eggs

2 cups of all-purpose flour

2 teaspoons of baking soda

2 teaspoons of ground cinnamon

1/2 teaspoon of ground ginger

1 teaspoon of baking powder

1/2 teaspoon of salt

2 cups of pumpkin puree or cooked,
  mashed pumpkin

1/2 cup of chopped pecans

Cinderella Cake with Princess Icing

INGREDIENTS

¹/₄ cup of Baked Butter (page 13)

¹/₂ cup of Chronic Cheese
   (page 41), room temperature

6 cups of icing sugar, sifted

2 tablespoons of orange juice

1 teaspoon of orange zest

PRINCESS ICING

Beat together the Chronic Cheese, Baked Butter, orange peel, and orange juice until smooth. Beat in the icing sugar, in increments, until blended and velvety smooth.

Cool in the fridge for about half an hour before icing the Cinderella cake.

Put about a third of the icing in between the 2 cake rounds and sprinkle with chopped pecans. Next, ice the top of the cake and finally ice the sides.

Cut the cake into 12 pieces. 1 piece is enough to get you baked.

Desserts

Candies

Almond Toffee

Easy to make and too easy to eat

Generously grease a 10 x 10-inch baking pan.

Combine the sugar, salt, water, and Baked Butter in a large pan and bring the mixture to a rolling boil.

Add about a third of the almonds and cook, stirring constantly to prevent the toffee from scorching, until the mixture reaches about 300° F (hard crack stage).

To make sure the mixture is at the hard crack stage, you can use a candy thermometer or get a clear drinking glass and fill it with cold water. Drop a little of the molten syrup into the cold water and if it's at the correct stage, will form hard, brittle threads that break when bent.

Remove the pan from the heat. Add the second third of almonds and stir them in. Pour the candy into the well-greased pan. Let the candy stand in a cool place until it hardens.

Remove the candy from the pan, spread the melted chocolate over the top, and sprinkle with the last remaining third of almonds. When the chocolate is firm, break the candy apart by tapping it with a sharp knife across the surface. A small handful of candy, about the size of a cookie, is enough to get you baked.

INGREDIENTS

½ cup of Baked Butter (page 13)

1 cup of chopped, blanched almonds

1 cup of sugar

½ teaspoon of salt

¼ cup of water

½ cup of melted milk chocolate chips

Chocolate Marshmallow Bites

For your sweet-toothed sweetheart

In a saucepan combine the Baked Butter, cream, sugar, and vanilla with 10 ounces of the semi-sweet chocolate. Bring the mixture to a slow boil and stir occasionally until it reaches the soft ball stage (238°F). If you don't have a candy thermometer then fill a clear glass with cold water. Drop the candy into the cold water. The candy should form a soft, flexible ball.

Remove the pot from the heat, add the marshmallows, and stir until thoroughly melted. Pour the mixture onto a well-greased baking sheet and spread evenly.

Allow the mixture to cool to the touch then break into bite-sized pieces. Roll each piece to form round, smooth balls. Place all balls back onto the cookie sheet and allow cooling for a good hour.

Melt the remaining semi-sweet chocolate in a double boiler or the microwave. Dip each ball in the melted chocolate and place back onto the cookie sheet. Let cool.

Melt the white chocolate in a double boiler or the microwave. Drizzle the melted white chocolate over the bites in a decorative fashion. Let cool. You'll make about 48 bites. 4 or 5 bites are enough to get you baked.

INGREDIENTS

2 cups of regular marshmallows

1½ teaspoons of pure vanilla extract

½ cup of Baked Butter (page 13)

4 cups of cream (18%)

4 cups of sugar

1 pound of semi-sweet chocolate, melted

4 ounces of white chocolate chips, melted

Peanut Butter Bites

Chock full of nutty goodness

Grease an 8 x 8-inch square pan.

Place the Baked Butter in a bowl and soften it with a wooden spoon. Blend in the corn syrup, peanut butter, salt, and vanilla, mixing until creamy. Stir in the icing sugar.

Turn the fudge onto a pastry board and knead until it's blended and smooth. Gradually add the chopped nuts if using, pressing and kneading them into the dough.

With greased fingers, press the fudge evenly into the prepared pan. Chill for at least 1 hour.

Cut into 16 serving-sized pieces. 1 or 2 pieces are enough to get you baked.

INGREDIENTS

¹/₂ cup of Baked Butter (page 13)

¹/₂ cup of light (or white) corn syrup

¹/₂ cup of peanut butter

¹/₂ teaspoon of salt

1 teaspoon of pure vanilla extract

3¹/₂ cups of sifted icing sugar (add more if the mixture is sticky)

³/₄ cup of chopped nuts (pecans or almonds or peanuts or a combination of all 3; or omit, depending on your taste)

Baked Fudge

Exceptionally rich in both chocolate and vanilla flavors

Grease a 10 x 10-inch square pan.

Combine the cocoa, sugar, and salt in a large saucepan. Add the milk gradually, mix thoroughly, and bring the mixture to a rapid boil on high heat, stirring continuously.

Turn the heat down to medium and continue to boil the mixture without stirring until it reaches a temperature of 236°F, the soft ball stage. When dropped into a bowl of very cold water, the mixture should form a soft ball, which flattens on removal from the water.

Remove the mixture from the heat. Add the Baked Butter and vanilla and then blend the mixture thoroughly until all the butter melts.

Allow the fudge to cool then cut it into 16 pieces. 1 piece is enough to get you baked.

To make vanilla fudge, just leave out the cocoa.

INGREDIENTS

1 1/2 cups of cocoa

6 cups of sugar

1/4 teaspoon of salt

3 cups of milk

1/2 cup of Baked Butter (page 13)

2 teaspoons of pure vanilla extract

Sesame Snaps

Melts in your mouth just like brittle!

Preheat the oven to 350°F. Grease a 13 x 9-inch baking pan. Spread the sesame seeds on baking sheet and toast in the oven for 15 minutes or until golden. Sprinkle half the seeds into baking pan. Reserve the rest. Set aside both.

In saucepan, bring the Baked Butter, brown sugar and water to boil, stirring constantly. Cook this mixture, stirring often, until it reaches 285°F (the soft crack stage). To make sure the mixture is at the soft crack stage, you can use a candy thermometer or get a clear drinking glass and fill it with cold water. Drop a little of the molten syrup into the cold water and if it's at the correct stage, it will form threads that are hard but not brittle.

Immediately remove the saucepan from the heat then stir in the baking soda as fast as possible. Pour the syrup over the toasted sesame seeds in the prepared pan. Allow it all to cool for at least 5 minutes.

Sprinkle the candy with the reserved seeds, pressing them lightly into the toffee. Be careful, hot candy can leave a bad burn. Let cool until firm.

Break the candy into pieces. It can be layered between waxed paper in an airtight container and stored for up to 1 month. A handful of candy, about the size of a cookie or a brownie, is enough to get you baked.

INGREDIENTS

- 1/2 cup of Baked Butter (page 13)
- 1/2 cup of sesame seeds
- 3/4 cup of packed brown sugar
- 1 1/2 tablespoons of water
- 1/3 teaspoon of baking soda

Butter Rum Fun

An alcohol-free treat with all the flavor of rum

Grease a 9 x 9-inch pan or large cookie sheet.

Mix the sugar, milk, and Baked Butter in a medium saucepan. Cook over medium heat, stirring frequently, until the mixture begins to form a soft ball. Remove the saucepan from the heat.

Add the chocolate chips, marshmallow crème, rum flavoring, and nuts. Stir the mixture quickly until well combined.

Pour onto the prepared pan or cookie sheet. Score the top immediately into 16 squares but don't cut the candy all the way through.

Allow the candy to cool thoroughly then finish cutting thorough the squares. 1 square is enough to get you baked.

INGREDIENTS

2 cups of sugar

³/₄ cup of evaporated milk

¹/₂ cup of Baked Butter (page 13)

¹/₂ cup of semi-sweet chocolate chips

1 cup of marshmallow créme

¹/₂ teaspoon of rum flavoring

1 cup of chopped cashews

Cool Mint Patties
Refreshing and euphoric

In a mixing bowl combine the corn syrup, peppermint extract, and Baked Butter. Stir in the sugar a little at a time. Add as much food coloring as you need to achieve your desired color and blend well.

Roll the mixture into 24 small balls. Place them a couple of inches apart on a cookie sheet that has been lined with wax paper. Use a fork to make each one flat.

Let the mint patties set in the refrigerator for several hours. Remove the patties from the refrigerator and let stand at room temperature for several days to dry out.

After a few days, transfer them to a container with an airtight lid and store them in the refrigerator.

3 or 4 patties are enough to get you baked.

INGREDIENTS

1/2 cup of light corn syrup

2 teaspoon of peppermint extract

1/2 cup of Baked Butter (page 13), softened

2 drops of food coloring (optional)

9 cups of powdered sugar, sifted

Orange Coconut Chews

A taste of the tropics in every bite

Preheat oven to 350°F. Grease a 9 x 9-inch pan.

In a saucepan, melt the Baked Butter then remove from the heat.

Stir in the brown sugar, vanilla, and orange rind. Once well combined, add the eggs.

In a bowl or on a piece of waxed paper combine the salt, flour and baking powder. Sift together three times. In a mixing bowl, combine the flour mixture with the butter mixture. Stir in the coconut and dates. Pour the batter into the prepared pan.

Bake for 25 to 30 minutes. Let cool and cut into 16 squares. If you'd like, roll each square into a ball and roll in more coconut.

1 square is enough to get you baked.

INGREDIENTS

$^1/_2$ cup of Baked Butter (page 13)

2 cups of brown sugar

2 slightly beaten eggs

2 teaspoons of pure vanilla extract

3 teaspoons of freshly grated orange rind

1 cup of flour

1 teaspoon of salt

2 teaspoons of baking powder

2 cups of shredded coconut

2 cups of chopped dates

Chocolate Chews

Chewy scrumptiousness for any chocolate lover

Preheat oven to 325°F. Grease an 8 x 8-inch pan.

In a bowl or on a piece of waxed paper, combine the all-purpose flour, salt, and sugar. Sift together 3 times. Set aside.

In a mixing bowl combine the Baked Butter, melted chocolate, vanilla, and egg, then beat well—over 200 strokes by hand or about 2 minutes with an electric hand mixer. With a spoon, stir in the oatmeal and the nuts. Spread the mixture evenly into the pan.

Bake for 30 minutes. Let cool thoroughly then cut into 12 squares. Roll each square into a ball and roll in sugar to coat .

1 chew is enough to get you baked.

INGREDIENTS

$^1/_2$ cup of Baked Butter (page 13)

$^1/_2$ cup of chocolate, melted

$^1/_2$ teaspoon of pure vanilla extract

$^3/_4$ cup of quick oats

$^1/_4$ cup of your favourite nuts, chopped

$^3/_4$ cup + 2 tablespoons of all-purpose flour, sifted

1 teaspoon of salt

$^3/_4$ cup of sugar

1 egg

Desserts

Gluten-Free

Sweet Shortbread

Short and sweet with just four ingredients

Preheat the oven to 300°F. Lightly grease a baking tray.

In a bowl, combine the cornstarch, icing sugar, and rice flour. Sift together 3 times. Add the Baked Butter, mix to combine then turn the dough out onto a floured surface and knead well.

Once the dough is soft, like mashed potatoes, knead for another 5 minutes. Place the dough, covered, into the refrigerator and leave for about an hour or so.

Take the dough out of the refrigerator and roll into 24 small balls, then press them lightly to make them flat. Place onto the baking tray and bake for 20 to 25 minutes, until the edges are ever so slightly browned.

Let cool for at least 10 minutes.

1 or 2 cookies are enough to get you baked.

INGREDIENTS

¹/₂ cup of cornstarch

¹/₂ cup of icing sugar

1 cup of rice flour

³/₄ cup of Baked Butter (page 13)

Cranberry Bread

Delicious with tea for an afternoon treat

Preheat the oven to 350°F. Grease and flour an 8 x 8-inch loaf pan (glass is best).

In a medium bowl, whisk together the gluten-free flour, salt, baking powder, and xanthan gum.

Using a mixer set on medium high, cream the Baked Butter and sugar until fluffy. Add the egg yolks and beat until combined.

Add the orange rind and a little of the flour. Mix. Add some orange juice. Mix. Repeat this process until the flour and orange juice are used up.

Turn off the mixer and stir in the cranberries using a wooden spoon.

Beat the egg whites in a separate bowl until stiff and then fold them gently into the batter.

Pour the batter into the loaf pan and place in the center of the oven. Bake for about 50 minutes, 60 if needed. The loaf should be golden in color.

Let cool, then cut the loaf into 12 slices. 1 slice is enough to get you baked. For an extra zing, spread Baked Butter on the slice before eating.

INGREDIENTS

2 cups of gluten-free flour mix

1 teaspoon of salt

5 teaspoons of baking powder (make sure it's gluten-free)

2 teaspoons of xanthan gum

1/2 cup of Baked Butter (page 13)

1/2 cup of sugar

3 eggs, separated

1/2 tablespoon of orange rind, grated

3/4 cup of orange juice (freshly squeezed is best)

1 cup of fresh cranberries, halved

Ginger Snap Cookies
Like a warm hug on a rainy afternoon

Preheat the oven to 350°F.

Cream together the Baked Butter, sugar, eggs, and molasses. Add the flour, salt, baking soda, cinnamon, ginger, allspice, and mix well.

Form into 1½-inch mud pies (like when you were a kid) and cover in sugar.

Place approximately 2 inches apart on a baking tray line with parchment paper.

Bake for 8 minute. Let cool.

1 or 2 cookies are enough to get you baked.

INGREDIENTS

¾ cup of Baked Butter (page 13), softened

1 cup of sugar

2 eggs

⅓ cup of blackstrap molasses

2¼ cups of buckwheat flour

¼ teaspoon of salt

2 teaspoons of baking soda

1½ tablespoons of ground cinnamon

1½ tablespoons of ground ginger

1½ teaspoons of ground allspice

Desserts

Sugar-Free

Chocolate Cookies

All the richness of chocolate with none of the sugar

Preheat the oven to 400°F.

Cream together the Baked Butter and sugar substitute. Add the eggs, vanilla, and milk and mix thoroughly.

Add half of the flour, mixing well, then stir in the melted chocolate. Add the rest of the flour and mix well.

Roll the dough into 16 small balls. Put flour on your hands to keep the dough from sticking to you. Press down with your fingers on the top of each cookie.

Bake for 10 minutes. Let cool.

1 or 2 cookies are enough to get you baked.

INGREDIENTS

¼ cup of sugar substitute like Equal

½ cup of Baked Butter (page 13)

2 eggs

1 teaspoon of pure vanilla extract

¼ cup of milk

2½ cups of cake flour

2 ounces (2 squares) of
    unsweetened chocolate, melted

Strawberry Cookies

A taste of summer that will leave you tickled pink

Preheat oven to 350°F.

In a bowl, cream together the Baked Butter and gelatin.

In another bowl, mix together the baking powder, flour, egg, and vanilla extract. Add this mixture to the butter mixture then beat with an electric mixer for about 2 minutes.

Roll out the dough and cut into squares. Place the cut cookies on an ungreased cookie sheet.

Bake for 10 to 12 minutes. Let cool.

1 to 2 cookies are enough to get you baked.

INGREDIENTS

1/2 cup of Baked Butter (page 13)

1 1/2 cups of flour

1/2 teaspoon of baking powder

1 package of strawberry gelatin

1 teaspoon of pure vanilla extract

1 egg

Peanut Butter Cookies

A traditional favorite that never fails to please

Preheat oven to 400°F. Grease a cookie sheet.

Mix together the Baked Butter, peanut butter, vanilla extract, maple syrup, and egg. Add the flour and baking powder. Beat well.

Roll the dough into 16 small balls. Place on the prepared baking sheet and flatten with a fork.

Bake for 8 to 10 minutes.

2 cookies are enough to get you baked.

INGREDIENTS

1 cup of flour

$^1/_2$ cup of Baked Butter (page 13)

$^1/_2$ cup of natural peanut butter

$^1/_3$ cup of sugar-free maple syrup

$^1/_2$ teaspoon of baking powder

1 teaspoon of pure vanilla extract

1 egg

Oatmeal Cookies

Natural oatmeal goodness
baked into every bite

Preheat the oven to 350°F. Lightly grease a cookie sheet.

Combine all the ingredients in a large bowl. Mix well.

Roll the dough into 16 small balls. Place on the prepared baking sheet and flatten with a fork.

Bake for 10 to 12 minutes or until the cookies turn golden brown.

2 cookies are enough to get you baked.

INGREDIENTS

¹/₂ cup of Baked Butter (page 13)

1 cup of flour

1 cup of oatmeal

1 cup of unsweetened applesauce

¹/₂ cup of raisins

1¹/₂ teaspoons of ground cinnamon

¹/₄ teaspoon of ground cloves

¹/₄ teaspoon of ground nutmeg

1 teaspoon of baking powder

¹/₂ teaspoon of baking soda

1 teaspoon of pure vanilla extract

¹/₄ cup of water

¹/₄ cup of chopped pecans

2 eggs

a pinch of salt

Banana Cookies

As moist and tender as classic banana bread

Preheat oven to 350°F.

Combine the bananas, oats, dates, Baked Butter, and vanilla and mix thoroughly. Allow the dough to rest for 20 minutes or so to let the flavors blend.

Drop the dough, a teaspoonful at a time, onto an ungreased cookie sheet and bake for 15 to 18 minutes or until golden brown.

2 cookies are enough to get you baked.

INGREDIENTS

3 bananas, smashed

2 cups of rolled oats

1 cup of chopped dates

1/2 cup of Baked Butter (page 13)

1 teaspoon of pure vanilla extract

Maple Cookies
Taste Canada with every bite!

Preheat oven to 375°F.

Cream together the Baked Butter, maple syrup, vanilla, and egg. Add the flour and stir until well combined.

Drop the dough, a teaspoonful at a time, onto an ungreased baking sheet.

Bake for 10 to 12 minutes, until the bottoms of cookies are golden brown—but just the bottom, not the top.

2 cookies are enough to get you baked.

INGREDIENTS

1/2 cup of Baked Butter (page 13)

1/2 cup of maple syrup

1 egg

1 teaspoon of pure vanilla extract

1 1/2 cups of flour

1/4 teaspoon of salt

Spice Bars

Wonderfully moist and not too sweet

Preheat oven to 350°F. Grease a 13 x 9-inch metal cake pan.

In large bowl, beat the Baked Butter with the granulated sugar substitute until fluffy. Beat the eggs into the mixture one at a time.

Whisk together the flour, cinnamon, baking soda, salt, and nutmeg. Stir flour mixture slowly into the butter mixture, alternating with the applesauce. Do this at least 2 times so that you're making at least 2 additions of each.

Stir in the raisins and almonds. Scoop the batter into the prepared cake pan.

Bake for about 40 minutes or until a toothpick can be inserted into the middle of the cake and come out clean. Let cool, then cut into about 16 bars.

1 bar is enough to get you baked.

INGREDIENTS

1/2 cup of Baked Butter (page 13), softened

3/4 cup of a granular sugar substitute like Splenda

1 1/2 cups of unsweetened applesauce

3 eggs

2 cups of cake flour

2 teaspoons of ground cinnamon

1/2 teaspoon of ground nutmeg

1/2 teaspoon of ground allspice

1 teaspoon of baking soda

1/2 teaspoon of salt

1 cup of raisins

1 cup of slivered almonds

Desserts

Vegan

Maple Oatmeal Chewies

A satisfying mouth feel and
a delicious taste

Preheat oven to 350°F.

Cream together the Baked Vegan Margarine, sugar, brown sugar, maple syrup, baby food, cornstarch, soy/almond milk, and vanilla in large bowl with an electric mixer on medium speed until well blended.

Combine the flour, baking soda and salt. Mix into the butter mixture. Stir in the oats, coconut, raisins, and walnuts.

Drop the dough, a teaspoonful at a time, onto an ungreased baking sheet.

Bake for 11 to 12 minutes for soft cookies, or 13 to 14 minutes for crispier cookies.

Remove the cookies to a cooling rack. This recipe should make about 36.

Two cookies are enough to get you baked.

INGREDIENTS

$1/2$ cup of Baked Vegan Margarine (page 13)

$1/2$ cup of brown sugar

$1/2$ cup of sugar

4 tablespoons of maple syrup

1 tablespoon of sweet potato baby food

1 teaspoon of cornstarch

2 tablespoons of soy/almond milk

1 teaspoon of pure vanilla extract

$1 1/4$ cups of flour

$1/2$ teaspoon of baking soda

$1/2$ cup of quick oats

$1/2$ cup of shredded, unsweetened coconut

$1/2$ cup of raisins

$1/2$ cup of walnut pieces

a pinch of salt

Butterscotch Brownies

Looks like a brownie, tastes like butterscotch pudding

Preheat oven to 350°F. Grease an 11 x 7-inch baking pan.

Melt the Baked Vegan Margarine in a large saucepan. Add the sugar and beat the two together until well mixed. Cool slightly, and then beat in the baby food, cornstarch, and vanilla.

Sift together the flour, salt and baking powder. Stir into the batter, then add the nuts. Mix well.

Spread the brownies in the pan and bake for 30 to 35 minutes or until a light golden color.

Cool in the pan for 10 minutes, and then turn out. This is easiest if you upend the pan over waxed paper, then turn the brownies right side up.

While the brownies are cooling, make the icing by creaming the margarine together with the icing sugar. Beat it until it's light, and then beat in the coffee mixture.

Spread the icing over the brownies. When the icing has set, cut the brownies into 24 squares. 1 square is enough to get you baked.

INGREDIENTS

1/2 cup of Baked Vegan Margarine (page 13), melted
1 cup of brown sugar
3 tablespoons of sweet potato baby food
1 1/2 teaspoons of cornstarch
1 teaspoon of pure vanilla extract
1 cup of flour
3/4 teaspoon of baking powder
1/2 cup of pecans, chopped
a pinch of salt

ICING

1/2 cup of vegan margarine
3 cups of sifted icing sugar
2 teaspoons of instant coffee, dissolved in 2 tablespoons hot water

Regular Special Brownies

The original "baked" dessert

Preheat the oven to 350°F. Grease an 8 x 8-inch pan.

In a medium bowl, combine the Melted Baked Margarine and cocoa powder and beat until the cocoa is completely dissolved. Blend in the sugar.

Add the egg replacer to the mixture until it is evenly dispersed throughout the mix. While beating (with an electric hand mixer), add the soy milk and vanilla extract a little at a time until it's all evenly mixed.

Sift together the flour, salt, and baking powder in a small bowl. Sift together 3 times.

Stir the flour mixture into the chocolate mixture with a spoon, just until the flour is totally incorporated. Do not overmix!

Fold in the chocolate chips. Spread the mixture in the pan and bake for 25 to 28 minutes. Cool completely before cutting into 16 squares.

1 brownie is enough to get you baked.

INGREDIENTS

1/2 cup of Baked Vegan Margarine (page 13), melted
1/2 cup of unsweetened cocoa
1 cup of sugar
egg replacer for 2 eggs
3 tablespoons of soy milk
2 teaspoons of pure vanilla extract
1/2 cup of flour
1/4 teaspoon of salt
1/4 teaspoon of baking powder
3/4 cup of vegan chocolate chips

Vegan Chocolate Chip Cookies

A vegan version of the all-time classic

Preheat oven to 350°F.

In a bowl, sift together the flour, salt, and baking soda and set aside.

In a separate large bowl, beat together the Baked Vegan Margarine, sugar, brown sugar, vanilla, and egg replacer.

Add the flour mixture to the margarine mixture and stir until the dough is combined well. Stir in the chocolate chips.

Drop the dough, a spoonful at a time, onto an ungreased cookie sheet. Bake for 8 to 10 minutes, until the edges are golden brown.

2 cookies are enough to get you baked.

INGREDIENTS

1 1/2 cups of flour

1/2 teaspoon of salt

1/2 teaspoon of baking soda

1/2 cup of Baked Vegan Margarine (page 13)

1/2 cup of brown sugar

1/2 cup of sugar

1/2 teaspoon of pure vanilla extract

egg replacer for 1 egg

1/2 cup of vegan chocolate chips

California Gold Bars
Jam-packed with the flavor of apricots

Preheat oven to 325°F. Grease a 9 x 9-inch pan.

Beat together the sugar, Baked Vegan Margarine, baby food, cornstarch, and vanilla until smooth and creamy. Stir in the flour and the nuts.

Spoon half the batter into the prepared pan. Spread it out evenly. Cover the batter evenly with jam. Cover the jam with the remaining batter.

Bake for 50 minutes. Cool for about 10 minutes. Cut into 24 bars.

1 bar is enough to get you baked.

INGREDIENTS

1/2 cup of brown sugar

1/2 cup of Baked Vegan Margarine (page 13)

1 tablespoon of apricot baby food

1/2 teaspoon of cornstarch

1/2 teaspoon of pure vanilla extract

1 cup of flour

1/2 cup of walnuts, chopped

1/4 cup of apricot jam

Gingerbread Cookies
Complex flavors with a fairytale ending

In a large bowl, beat together the Baked Vegan Margarine and sugar. Add the egg replacer, molasses, and vinegar, and set aside.

In a separate bowl, sift together the flour, salt, baking soda, ginger, cinnamon, cloves, and nutmeg. Stir the flour mixture into the margarine mixture until it's well combined.

Refrigerate the dough for at least 2 hours or overnight. This will help the mixture become firm.

Preheat the oven to 375°F.

Form the cookie mixture into 1/2-inch balls and flatten. Place onto a cookie sheet and bake for 6–8 minutes. Let cool.

2 cookies are enough to get you baked.

INGREDIENTS

1/2 cup of Baked Vegan Margarine (page 13)

1/2 cup of sugar

egg replacer for 1 egg

1/2 cup of molasses

1 tablespoon of apple cider vinegar

2 1/2 cups of flour

1/4 teaspoon of salt

1 teaspoon of baking soda

1 teaspoons of ground ginger

1 teaspoon of ground cinnamon

1/2 teaspoon of ground cloves

1/2 teaspoon of ground nutmeg

Molasses Cookies
Fiery, chewy, and totally dairy-free

In a large bowl, sift together the baking soda, sugar, ginger, salt, flour, and cornstarch, then cut in the Baked Vegan Margarine.

Add the molasses and the baby food and mix well. Form the dough into a log and refrigerate for at least an hour.

Preheat the oven to 375°F.

Cut the dough into quarter-inch slices. Lay the slices on a cookie sheet and bake for 8-10 minutes. Let cool.

While they're cooling make a glaze with the combination of powdered sugar, vanilla, and tablespoons milk. Drizzle the glaze over the cookies.

2 cookies are enough to get you baked.

INGREDIENTS

1/2 cup of Baked Vegan Margarine {page 13}

1/3 cup of molasses

1/2 teaspoon of baking soda

2 cups of brown sugar

1/4 teaspoon of ground ginger

1/4 teaspoon of salt

3/4 cup of flour

1 tablespoon of sweet potato baby food

1/2 teaspoon of cornstarch

GLAZE

2 cups of powdered sugar

1 teaspoon of vanilla extract

3 tablespoons of milk

Lemon Poppy Seed Cookies

So rich and moist, 1 is never enough

Preheat oven to 350°F.

Cream together the sugar, brown sugar, and Baked Vegan Margarine until smooth and creamy. Add the soy yogurt and vanilla and mix thoroughly.

Add the baking soda, salt, lemon zest, flour, and poppy seeds. Mix well. Drop the dough, a tablespoonful at a time, onto a cookie sheet. Bake for 8 minutes.

2 cookies are enough to get you baked.

INGREDIENTS

- 3/4 cup of sugar
- 3/4 cup of brown sugar
- 1/2 cup of Baked Vegan Margarine (page 13)
- 1 cup of soy yogurt
- 1 1/2 teaspoons of pure vanilla extract
- 3/4 teaspoon of baking soda
- 3/4 teaspoon of salt
- 1 teaspoon of lemon zest
- 2 1/2 cups of flour
- 3/4 cup of poppy seeds

Coco Nutty Lime Cookies

Inspired by the tastes of Asia

Preheat oven to 375°F.

Cream the Baked Vegan Margarine, icing sugar, vanilla, coconut extract, lime juice, and lime zest in a large bowl until smooth. Gradually add in the cornstarch and flour, beating after each addition.

Stir in the ¹/₂ cup of coconut, kneading it in if necessary. If the dough is crumbling, add a touch more lime juice or a splash of soy milk. Roll the dough into balls, about 2 tablespoons of dough each.

Pour the remaining coconut into a small bowl. Roll each cookie in the coconut and place on a parchment-lined cookie sheet. Sprinkle the rest of the coconut on top of the cookies.

Bake cookies for about 15 minutes or until firm with golden brown bottoms. Let the cookies sit on the cookie tray for at least 10 minutes before moving them to a cooling rack or they will crumble when you transfer them.

Make the lime glaze by combining all ingredients together in a small bowl and stirring until smooth.

When the cookies are almost completely cooled, dip each one in the glaze and let them sit until dry. 2 cookies are enough to get you baked.

INGREDIENTS

¹/₂ cup of Baked Vegan Margarine (page 13)

¹/₄ cup of icing sugar

¹/₄ teaspoon of pure vanilla extract

¹/₄ teaspoon of coconut extract

1 tablespoon of lime juice

¹/₄ teaspoon of lime zest

¹/₂ cup of cornstarch

³/₄ cup of flour

¹/₂ cup + ²/₃ cup of sweetened shredded coconut

LIME GLAZE

2 tablespoons of lime juice

¹/₂ cup of icing sugar

¹/₄ teaspoon of coconut extract

Fruity Loopy Shortbread

A taste of Christmas for your inner fruitcake

Preheat the oven to 375°F.

Whisk together the flour, baking soda, ginger, nutmeg, cinnamon, and cream of tartar.

In a large bowl, beat the Baked Vegan Margarine and sugar until fluffy. Add the baby food and cornstarch. Stir in the vanilla and candied fruit.

Add the flour mixture to the margarine mixture. Mix well. Roll the stiff dough into 1-inch balls. Place the balls on an ungreased cookie sheet, then flatten ever so slightly.

Bake for 10 to 12 minutes or until slightly brown on the edges. Remove from the oven and then cover them with a glaze of icing sugar, soy milk/almond milk, and vanilla while they're still warm if you want some extra sweetness.

3 cookies are enough to get you baked.

INGREDIENTS

1 1/4 cup of flour
1/2 teaspoon of cream of tartar
3/4 cup of icing sugar
1 cup of candied fruit
1/2 teaspoon of ground ginger
1/2 teaspoon of ground nutmeg
1/2 teaspoon of ground cinnamon
1 teaspoon of pure vanilla extract
1/2 teaspoon of baking soda
1/2 cup of Baked Vegan Margarine (page 13), softened
1 tablespoon of sweet potato baby food
1/2 teaspoon of cornstarch

Drinks

Martini

Shaken, not stirred—although you will be!

Into a mixing glass, toss in the 6 ice cubes then pour in the Ganja Gin and the vermouth.

Stir well.

Strain and pour into a martini glass.

To finish, either drop a couple of green olives into the bottom of the martini glass, or arrange a twist of lemon peel on the edge of the martini glass.

For every alcoholic beverage you drink make sure you drink a pint of water—and this goes for alcohol without weed in it, too!

1 Martini should be more than enough to get you baked.

INGREDIENTS

2 ounces of Ganga Gin made via
    the Alcohol Extraction method
    (page 29)
1/4 ounce of dry vermouth
1 to 3 green olives OR a twist of
    lemon peel
6 ice cubes

Cardinale

The perfect mix of bud and bitters

Fill an old fashioned glass with ice. Pour all ingredients over the ice and serve.

For every alcoholic beverage you drink make sure you drink a pint of water—and this goes for alcohol without weed in it, too!

1 Cardinale should be more than enough to get you baked.

INGREDIENTS

2 ounces of Ganga Gin made via the Alcohol Extraction method (page 29)

1/2 ounce of dry vermouth

1/2 ounce of Cannabis Campari made via the Alcohol Extraction method (page 29)

ice

Americano

A sip of home with the taste of Italy!

Fill a medium-sized tumbler or a highball glass with ice. Pour the Cannabis Campari and the vermouth into the tumbler. Top the glass off with club soda.

Garnish with a lemon twist or a slice of orange.

For every alcoholic beverage you drink make sure you drink a pint of water—and this goes for alcohol without weed in it, too!

1 Americano should be more than enough to get you baked.

INGREDIENTS

1 ounce of Cannabis Campari made via the Alcohol Extraction method (page 29)

1 ounce of sweet vermouth

club soda

a lemon twist or orange slice for garnish

ice

Negroni
The flavor of Florence

Fill a highball glass three quarters of the way with ice; cracked ice works best. Pour all the ingredients over the ice. You can add a splash of club soda but it's optional.

Garnish with the blood orange slice.

For every alcoholic beverage you drink make sure you drink a pint of water—and this goes for alcohol without weed in it, too!

1 Negroni should be more than enough to get you baked.

1 ounce of Ganga Gin made via the Alcohol Extraction method (page 29)

1 ounce of sweet vermouth

1 ounce of Cannabis Campari made via the Alcohol Extraction method (page 29)

ice

slice of blood orange

Laced Limoncello

Not the lemonade your grandma used to make!

Shave off the yellow part of the lemon rinds using a potato peeler. Put these lemon rinds in a large glass bottle or jar and add the Vector Vodka.

Cover the bottle or jar with plastic wrap as well as the lid to prevent any alcohol from evaporating. Let the bottle sit for 2 weeks at room temperature.

Boil the water in a large saucepan. Remove the pan from the heat and add sugar. Stir until all the sugar has dissolved and let the mixture cool.

Strain the lemon rinds from the 2-week-old Vector Vodka mix. Add the vodka to the sugared water.

Fill the bottle or jar back up with the new mixture and cover with plastic wrap as well as the lid. Set the bottle aside for an additional 10 days, again at room temperature.

After 10 days, the Laced Limoncello is ready. It is best served chilled.

For every alcoholic beverage you drink make sure you drink a pint of water—and this goes for alcohol without weed in it, too!

1 glass should be enough to get one person baked.

INGREDIENTS

8 cups of Vector Vodka made via the Alcohol Extraction method (page 29)
20 lemons (Sorrento lemons, if possible)
4 cups of sugar
4 cups of water

Angelo Azzurro

A blue dream over ice

Pour the ingredients into a cocktail shaker and shake well. Serve in an ice-filled rock glass or a Martini glass. No garnish needed.

For every alcoholic beverage you drink, make sure you drink a pint of water—and this goes for alcohol without weed in it, too!

1 glass should be enough to get one person baked.

2 ounces of Ganga Gin made via the Alcohol Extraction method (page 29)
1 ounce of Triple Sec or Cointreau
1/2 ounce of Blue Curacao

Laced Lemon Martini

Everyone's favorite drink laced with a little lemon

Pour the ingredients into a cocktail shaker filled with ice and shake well. Serve in a Martini glass with a lemon twist as garnish.

For every alcoholic beverage you drink make sure you drink a pint of water—and this goes for alcohol without weed in it, too!

1 glass should be enough to get one person baked.

INGREDIENTS

½ ounce of Laced Limoncello

1 ounce of Vector Vodka made via the Alcohol Extraction method (page 29)

1 lemon twist

Hazelnut Martini

You'll go nuts for this version of a classic cocktail!

Rim a Martini glass with brown sugar.

Pour the ingredients into a cocktail shaker filled with ice and shake well. Strain into a Martini glass and garnish with an orange slice.

For every alcoholic beverage you drink make sure you drink a pint of water—and this goes for alcohol without weed in it, too!

1 glass should be enough to get one person baked.

1¼ ounces of Vector Vodka made via the Alcohol Extraction method (page 29)

¾ ounce of Frangelico

¾ ounce of Cointreau

1 ounce of half-and-half

Caffé Polonaise

A drink with a tang!

Put the 2 sugar cubes in a coffee cup or espresso cup.

Add the Vector Vodka, coffee, and lemon juice to the cup and stir.

If you're using the cream, float it; do not stir or mix it.

For every alcoholic beverage you drink make sure you drink a pint of water—and this goes for alcohol without weed in it, too!

1 glass should be enough to get 1 person baked.

INGREDIENTS

1 ounce of Vector Vodka made via the Alcohol Extraction method (page 29)

1 cup of coffee or a demitasse of espresso

1 teaspoon of lemon juice

2 sugar cubes

cream (optional)

Caffé Bella

Just the thing for an afternoon pick-me-up!

Place the Vector Vodka, Frangelico, Irish cream liqueur, and coffee into an espresso cup and stir.

If you're using the cream, float it; do not stir or mix it.

For every alcoholic beverage you drink make sure you drink a pint of water—and this goes for alcohol without weed in it, too!

1 glass should be enough to get 1 person baked.

INGREDIENTS

1 ounce of Vector Vodka made via the Alcohol Extraction method (page 29)

1/2 ounce of Frangelico

1/2 ounce of Irish cream liqueur

1 demitasse of espresso

cream (optional)

Caffé Pucci

A treat served warm, and sure
to melt the coldest of hearts

Put the brown sugar in an espresso cup.

Add the Vector Vodka, almond liqueur and the coffee and stir.

If you are using the cream, float it; do not stir or mix it.

For every alcoholic beverage you drink make sure you drink a pint of water—and this goes for alcohol without weed in it, too!

1 glass should be enough to get 1 person baked.

INGREDIENTS

1 ounce of Vector Vodka made via the Alcohol Extraction method (page 29)

$1/2$ ounce of almond liqueur

1 teaspoon of brown sugar

1 demitasse of espresso

cream (optional)

The Mojito
Minty rum fun

INGREDIENTS

1 cup of boiling water

1 box of lime Jell-o

6 ounces of Wasted White Rum made via the Alcohol
  Extraction method (page 29)

2 ounces of cold water

chopped mint leaves

Pour the boiling water into a bowl. Dissolve the lime Jell-o in the water and stir until fully dissolved. Add the Wasted White Rum and cold water. Stir well and cool before pouring into Jell-o shot cups. Top each shooter with a mint leaf if desired. Allow to set. 1 Mojito shot is enough to get you baked.

The Daiquiri
Summer in a shot glass!

INGREDIENTS

1 cup of boiling water

1 box of wild strawberry Jell-o

6 ounces of Wasted White Rum made via the Alcohol
  Extraction method (page 29)

1 ounce of margarita mix or frozen limeade

fresh strawberries, sliced

Pour the boiling water into a bowl. Dissolve the wild strawberry Jell-o in the boiling water and stir until fully dissolved. Add the Wasted White Rum and margarita mix or limeade, then top with the strawberries. Stir well and cool before pouring into Jell-o shot cups. Top each shooter with a slice of strawberry if desired. Allow to set. 1 Daiquiri shot is enough to get you baked.

The Apple Jack
One for autumn

The Bolt of Lightning
Thunderously good!

INGREDIENTS

1 1/2 cups of boiling water

2 boxes of lemon Jell-o

1/2 cup of Wasted White Rum made via the Alcohol
    Extraction method (page 29)

1/2 cup of sweet vermouth

1/4 cup of apple brandy

1/4 cup of grenadine

dried apple slices

Pour the boiling water into a bowl. Dissolve the lemon
Jell-o in the water and stir until fully dissolved. Add
the cold water, Wasted White Rum, sweet vermouth,
apple brandy, and grenadine, then top with the dried
apple slices. Stir well and cool before pouring into
Jell-o shot cups. Top each shooter with a dried apple
slice if desired. Allow to set. 1 Apple Jack shot is
enough to get you baked.

INGREDIENTS

1 cup of boiling water

1 box of orange Jell-o

1/2 cup of Red Bull

1/4 cup of Wasted White Rum made via the Alcohol
    Extraction method (page 29)

1/4 cup of blue curacao

orange slices, cut into quarters

Pour the boiling water into a bowl. Dissolve the
orange Jell-o in the water and stir until fully
dissolved. Add the Red Bull, Wasted White Rum,
and blue curacao, then top with the orange quarters.
Stir well and cool before pouring into Jell-o shot cups.
Top each shooter with an orange slice if desired.
Allow to set. 1 Bolt of Lightning shot is enough to get
you baked.

Banana Split
1 of your 5 a day

The Gummy Worm
Takes you right back to childhood

INGREDIENTS

1 cup of boiling water

1 box of strawberry Jell-o

1/4 cup of cold water

1/4 cup of Vector Vodka made via the Alcohol Extraction method (page 29)

1/4 cup of banana liqueur

1/4 cup of Crème de Cacao

maraschino cherries

Pour the boiling water into a bowl. Dissolve the strawberry Jell-o in the water and stir until fully dissolved. Add the cold water, Vector Vodka, banana liqueur, and Crème de Cacao, stir. Stir well and cool before pouring into Jell-o shot cups. Top each shooter with a cherry if desired. Allow to set. 1 Banana Split shot is enough to get you baked.

INGREDIENTS

2 1/4 cups of boiling water

3 boxes of any flavor Jell-o

2 cups of Vector Vodka made via the Alcohol Extraction method (page 29)

3/4 cup of ice cold water

1 gummy worm to each shooter

Pour the boiling water into a bowl. Dissolve the Jell-o in the water and stir until fully dissolved. Add the cold water, Vector Vodka, and stir. Let cool before pouring into Jell-o shot cups and top each shot with a gummy worm. Allow to set. 1 Gummy Worm shot is enough to get you baked.

The Melon Baller
Everyone wants to be a baller!

INGREDIENTS

1 cup of boiling water

1 box of orange Jell-o

1/4 cup of cold water

1/2 cup of Wasted White Rum made via the Alcohol
   Extraction method (page 29)

1/4 cup of melon liqueur

freshly scooped melon balls

Pour the boiling water into a bowl. Dissolve the Jell-o in the water and stir until fully dissolved. Add the cold water, Wasted White Rum, and melon liqueur and stir. Let cool before pouring into Jell-o shot cups and top each shot with a melon ball. Allow to set. 1 Melon Baller shot is enough to get you baked.

The Cherry Bomb
A blast of energy

INGREDIENTS

1 cup of Red Bull

1 box of cherry Jell-o

1 cup of Vector Vodka made via the Alcohol Extraction
   method (page 29)

maraschino cherries

Boil the Red Bull and pour into a bowl. Dissolve the cherry Jell-o in the Red Bull and stir until fully dissolved. Add the Vector Vodka. Stir well and cool before pouring into Jell-o shot cups; top with maraschino cherry. Allow to set. 1 Cherry Bomb shot is enough to get you baked.

Index

Index